Guided Math Les_____
in Third Grade

Guided Math Lessons in Third Grade provides detailed lessons to help you bring guided math groups to life. Based on the bestselling *Guided Math in Action*, this practical book offers 16 lessons, taught in a round of three—concrete, pictorial and abstract. The lessons are based on the priority standards and cover fluency, word problems, fractions and place value. Author Dr. Nicki Newton shows you the content as well as the practices and processes that should be worked on in the lessons, so that students not only learn the content but also how to solve problems, reason, communicate their thinking, model, use tools, use precise language, and see structure and patterns.

Throughout the book, you'll find tools, templates and blackline masters so that you can instantly adapt the lesson to your specific needs and use it right away. With the easy-to-follow plans in this book, students can work more effectively in small guided math groups—and have loads of fun along the way! Remember that guided math groups are about doing the math. So throughout these lessons you will see students working with manipulatives to make meaning, doing mathematical sketches to show what they understand and can make sense of the abstract numbers. When students are given the opportunities to make sense of the math in hands-on and visual ways, then the math begins to make sense to them!

Dr. Nicki Newton has been an educator for 30 years, working both nationally and internationally with students of all ages. She has worked on developing Math Workshop and Guided Math Institutes around the country; visit her website at www.drnickinewton.com. She is also an avid blogger (www.guidedmath.wordpress.com), tweeter (@drnickimath) and Pinterest pinner (www.pinterest.com/drnicki7).

Guided Math Lessons in Third Grade

Getting Started

Dr. Nicki Newton

Routledge
Taylor & Francis Group

NEW YORK AND LONDON

First published 2022
by Routledge
605 Third Avenue, New York, NY 10158

and by Routledge
2 Park Square, Milton Park, Abingdon, Oxon, OX14 4RN

Routledge is an imprint of the Taylor & Francis Group, an informa business

Library of Congress Cataloging-in-Publication Data
A catalog record for this book has been requested

ISBN: 978-0-367-77051-8 (hbk)
ISBN: 978-0-367-76001-4 (pbk)
ISBN: 978-1-003-16954-3 (ebk)

DOI: 10.4324/9781003169543

Typeset in Palatino
by Apex CoVantage, LLC

Contents

Meet the Author

Dr. Nicki Newton has been an educator for over 30 years, working both nationally and internationally, with students of all ages. Having spent the first part of her career as a literacy and social studies specialist, she built on those frameworks to inform her math work. She believes that math is intricately intertwined with reading, writing, listening and speaking. She has worked on developing Math Workshop and Guided Math Institutes around the country. Most recently, she has been helping districts and schools nationwide to integrate their State Standards for Mathematics and think deeply about how to teach these within a math workshop model. Dr. Nicki works with teachers, coaches and administrators to make math come alive by considering the powerful impact of building a community of mathematicians who make meaning of real math together. When students do real math, they learn it. They own it, they understand it, and they can do it. Every one of them. Dr. Nicki is also an avid blogger (www.guidedmath.word press.com), tweeter (@drnickimath) and Pinterest pinner (www.pinterest.com/drnicki7/). She speaks around the country and will virtually pop into any bookstudy if requested!

Contact her at:
Phone: 347–688–4927
Email: drnicki7@gmail.com

Find More Online!

Resources, videos and conversations with Dr. Nicki can be found in the Guided Math Dropbox Resources: https://bit.ly/2Ja4sMY

Acknowledgments

I thank God for life and happiness. I thank my family and friends for all their support. I thank my editor Lauren who is the best in the world! I thank all the reviewers who gave feedback that helped make the series what it is! I thank the copyediting and production team for all their hard work.

I would also like to thank Math Learning Center (www.mathlearningcenter.org/apps), Braining Camp (www.brainingcamp.com/) and Didax (www.didax.com/math/virtual-manipulatives.html) for the use of screenshots of their fabulous virtual manipulatives.

www.brainingcamp.com/
www.mathlearningcenter.org/apps

1

Introduction

Figure 1.1 Guided Math Example

I pull a group of 3rd graders who are working on multiplying by 5. We are looking at the strategy of using our ten facts to help us with our 5 facts. We are playing a bump game. When they pull a 5 fact, they are encouraged to not just skip count by 5's but to think of their 10 facts and half it.

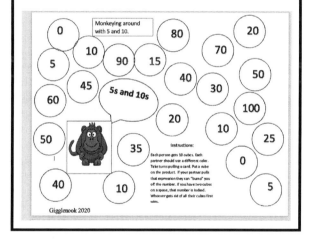

Figure 1.2 Guided Math Example 2

I pull a different group who is working on arrays. They are playing a game where they each pull a card and whoever has the largest product wins. They have a visual scaffold on their flashcard.

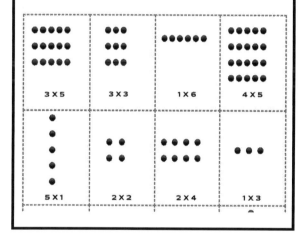

Guided math is a small group instructional strategy that teaches students in their zone of proximal development around the priority standards (see Figures 1.1 and 1.2). There are so many standards, but every state has priority focus standards. Those are the standards that you teach in a small guided math group. It is a time for hands-on, minds-on learning based on the standards. It is a time for discussing ideas, listening to the thinking of others, reasoning out loud and becoming a confident, competent mathematician.

Guided math groups are for everyone! Too often, students are rushed through big ideas, understandings and skills. They are left with ever widening gaps. Guided math groups give teachers the time needed to work with students in a way that they can all learn. Guided math groups can be used to remediate, to teach on grade level concepts and to address the needs of students who are working beyond grade level.

DOI: 10.4324/9781003169543-1

Figure 1.3 Visually Leveled Flashcards   **Figure 1.4** Number Line

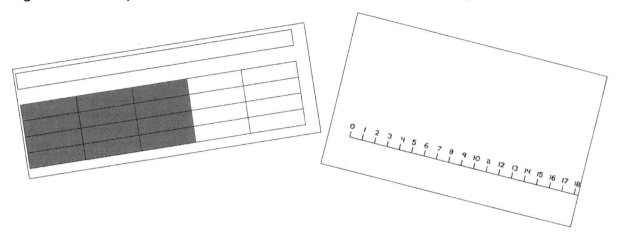

There are different ways that students can be grouped. Sometimes students are grouped by readiness. Other times students are grouped by interest or choice. So, for example, say you are working on rounding and half the class gets it and the other half is still struggling. You might pull some temporary small groups and practice some hands-on lessons with the beaded number line for the students who are struggling, but that doesn't mean you will forget about the other kids. You could also pull another group of kids and play a rounding card game (they are past needing the concrete scaffolds). You could have days where you pull a heterogeneous group and allow the kids who need the scaffolds to use them during the game (see Figures 1.3 and 1.4).

You could also ask students what they are interested in working on in small groups. You all would have a whole class discussion and generate a list of topics and then students would sign up for groups sessions that they are interested in attending. The focus here is that the students generate the topics and then sign up for them. Another way to do this is to have the teacher think about different topics that the students need to work on, based on the data and then offer those topics to the students, and they can sign up for which sessions that they want to attend.

Guided math groups can be heterogeneous or homogeneous. It depends on what you are trying to do. If you are teaching a specific skill, such as multiplying by 4's, one group could be working with visually leveled flashcards and another group could be working with more abstract number flashcards. You could also pull a group that is still exploring it just concretely on the beaded number line for another session. The groups are flexible and students work in different groups at different times, never attached to any one group for the entire year. Students meet in a particular guided math group for three or four times based on their specific instructional needs and then they move on.

Guided math groups can occur in all types of classrooms. Typically, they are part of a math workshop. In a math workshop (see Figure 1.5) there are three parts.

Opening
♦ Energizers and routines
♦ Problem solving
♦ Mini-lesson

Student Activity
♦ Math workstations
♦ Guided math groups

Debrief
♦ Discussion
♦ Exit slip
♦ Mathematician's chair share

Figure 1.5 Math Workshop

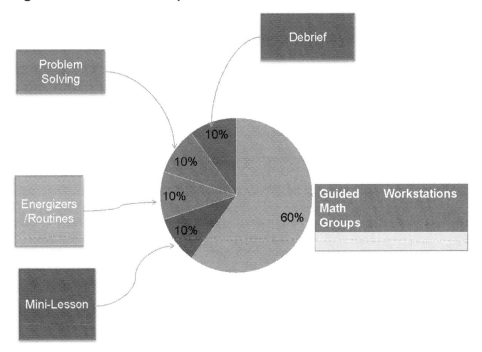

What Are the Other Kids Doing?

The other students should be engaged in some type of independent practice. They can be working alone, with partners or in small groups. They could be rotating through stations based on a designated schedule, or they could be working from a menu of Must Do's and Can Do's. The point is that students should be practicing fluency, word problems and place value and working on items in the current unit of study. This work should be organized in a way that students are working on in their zone of proximal development (Vygotsky, 1978).

Differentiating workstations helps to purposefully plan for the learning of all students (see Figures 1.6 and 1.7). For example, the fluency workstation games should be divided by strategy; some, students can be working on either make 10 facts, doubles, or bridge 10 facts, depending on what they need (Baroody, 2006; Van de Walle & Lovin, 2006; Henry & Brown, 2008). Another example is word problems. There are different types of word problems, and they range from easy to increasingly challenging. Knowing the learning trajectories and understanding the structures that go from simple to complex can help organize the teaching and learning of word problems (Carpenter, Fennema, Franke, Levi, & Empson, 1999/2015; Fuchs et al., 2010); Jitendra, Hoff, & Beck (1999) (Figure 1.8).

Benefits of Guided Math Groups

♦ See student knowledge in action
♦ Monitor the concepts and skills that are understood
♦ Catch and address the misunderstandings
♦ Ask questions that highlight thinking

Figures 1.6 & **1.7** Workstation Games

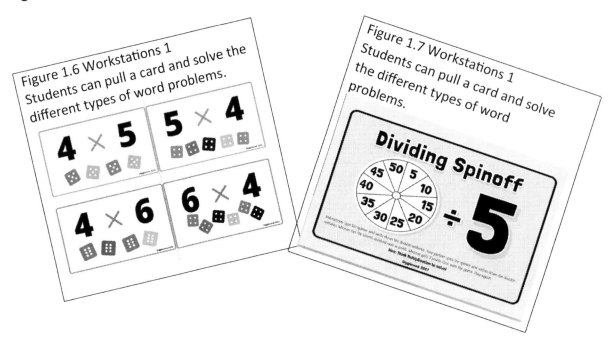

Figure 1.6 Workstations 1 Students can pull a card and solve the different types of word problems.

Figure 1.7 Workstations 1 Students can pull a card and solve the different types of word problems.

- ♦ Analyze thinking
- ♦ Listen to conversations
- ♦ Assess in the moment
- ♦ Redirect in the moment
- ♦ Differentiate as needed

Key Points

- ♦ Different reasons: remediate, focus on grade level topics or working beyond grade level
- ♦ Cycle of engagement: concrete, pictorial, abstract
- ♦ Heterogeneous and homogeneous grouping
- ♦ Math workshop
- ♦ Math workstations
- ♦ Benefits of guided math

Chapter Summary

Guided math is a great way to differentiate learning for all your students. Focus on the priority standards. Students approach these standards through a concrete, pictorial and abstract cycle of engagement. Sometimes, the groups are homogeneous groups, and other times the groups are heterogeneous. Guided math groups can be done in a variety of ways, either traditional set-ups or a math workshop model. The other students should always be doing work that they are familiar with and are practicing in the math workstation or on menus. Many times, the work that students are working on in the guided math group is carried over into the math workstation. When the students are in guided math groups, the other students should be meaningfully engaged in math workstations or working on menu activities. All of this works together to give all students a chance to learn.

Figure 1.8 Workstation Contract

Workstation Contract

I have the privilege of learning with the Math Workstations.

I will play fair.

I will be a good sport. If I win, I will celebrate appropriately. If I lose, I'll be a good sport.

I will use the math manipulatives the way they are supposed to be used.

I will use the digital resources the way they are supposed to be used.

I will put everything back neatly.

I will work hard every day.

I will keep trying when the going gets tough!

My Signature:_____

Date: _____

Reflection Questions

1. How are you differentiating instruction around the priority standards right now?
2. Currently, how do you group students? What informs your grouping?
3. Do you have a plan to make sure that everybody fully understands the priority standards?

References

Baroody, A. J. (2006). Why children have difficulties mastering the basic number combinations and how to help them. *Teaching Children Mathematics, 13*, 22–32.

Carpenter, T. P., Fennema, E., Franke, M. L., Levi, L., & Empson, S. B. (2015). *Children's mathematics: Cognitively guided instruction*. NH: Heinemann.

Fuchs, L., Zumeta, R., Schumacher, R., Powell, S., Seethaler, P., Hamlett, C., & Fuchs, D. (2010). The effects of schema-broadening instruction on second graders' word-problem performance and their ability to represent word problems with algebraic equations: A randomized control study. *Elementary School Journal, 110*(4), 446–463. Retrieved January 4, 2020 from https://www.ncbi.nlm.nih.gov/pubmed/20539822

Henry, V., & Brown, R. (2008, March). First-grade basics: An investigation into teaching and learning of an accelerated, high-demand memorization standard. *Journal for Research in Mathematics Education, 39*(2), 153–183.

Jitendra, A. K., Hoff, K., & Beck, M. M. (1999). Teaching middle school students with learning disabilities to solve word problems using a schema-based approach. *Remedial and Special Education, 20*(1), 50–64. https://doi.org/10.1177/074193259902000108

Van de Walle, J. A., & Lovin, L. A. H. (2006). *Teaching student-centered mathematics: Grades 3–5*. Boston: Pearson.

Vygotsky, L. S. (1978). *Mind in society: The development of higher psychological processes*. Cambridge, MA: Harvard University Press.

2

Behind the Scenes

Assessment

Assessment is a crucial element in designing a guided math lesson. Teachers have to know where their students are along the trajectory of learning so that they can plan to teach them purposefully. Teachers need actionable data. Actionable data is data that can be used immediately to develop meaningful lessons. At the beginning of the year, teachers need to get data about the priority standards/major cluster standards from the year before so they can figure out if there are any gaps and make a plan to close them. Richardson notes, "The information gathered from the assessments helps teachers pinpoint what each child knows and still needs to learn. They are not about 'helping children be right,' but about uncovering their instructional needs." (n.d.)

Math Running Records is a great way to check fluency! It's the GPS of fact fluency (Figure 2.1). Remember, every summer, students lose 2.6 months of math at least (Shafer, 2016). Teachers should assess fluency, word problems, operations and algebraic thinking and place value in the beginning of the year. At the middle of the year, teachers should assess all the grade level work done in these areas during the first part of the year. At the end of the year, teachers should assess all the priority standards for the grade. Throughout the year, teachers should rely on entrance and exit slips, quizzes, anecdotes, unit assessments and conferring to get information about students (Figure 2.2).

Grouping

Guided math groups should have three to five students. Sometimes they are heterogeneous groups, and sometimes they are homogeneous groups. It depends on what you are trying to do. If you are working on big ideas and understanding, you might pull a small group of students and have them work on modeling with different tools. You might pull students together and work on some word problems. However, if you are working on multiplication basic facts and you are working on a specific strategy, you might pull a group that is working on relating the 2's, 4's and 8's. You might pull another group that you work with on using the doubles facts. Groups should last between 10 and 15 minutes. Remember the attention span rule: age plus a few minutes.

Differentiation

After teachers get the data, they need to use it to differentiate (see Figure 2.1). Some of the work is to close the gaps. Some of the work is to accelerate the learning of the advanced students. Some of the work is to teach in the grade level zone. A big part of the differentiation aspect of guided math lessons is the concrete, pictorial and abstract cycle. Sometimes, students know the answer but do not necessarily understand the math. It is crucial to do quick assessments with

DOI: 10.4324/9781003169543-2

Figure 2.1 Math Running Records

Addition Running Record Recording Sheet

Student: _____ Teacher: _____ Date: _____

Part 1: Initial Observations
Teacher: We are now going to administer Part 1 of the Running Record. I am going to give you a sheet of paper with some problems. I want you to go from the top to the bottom and tell me just the answer. If you get stuck, you can stop and ask for what you need to help you. If you want to pass, you can. We might not do all of the problems. I am going to take notes so I remember what happened. Let's start.

Part 1	Codes: What do you notice?	Initial Observations of Strategies	Data Code Names
0 + 1 a 5s pth	ca fco cah coh wo sc asc dk	0 1 2 3 4M 4	A0----- add 0
2 + 1 a 5s pth	ca fco cah coh wo sc asc dk	0 1 2 3 4M 4	A1----- add 1
3 + 2 a 5s pth	ca fco cah coh wo sc asc dk	0 1 2 3 4M 4	Aw5--- add w/in 5
2 + 6 a 5s pth	ca fco cah coh wo sc asc dk	0 1 2 3 4M 4	Aw10—add w/in 10
4 + 6 a 5s pth	ca fco cah coh wo sc asc dk	0 1 2 3 4M 4	AM10---add making 10
10 + 4 a 5s pth	ca fco cah coh wo sc asc dk	0 1 2 3 4M 4	A10-----add 10 to a #
7 + 7 a 5s pth	ca fco cah coh wo sc asc dk	0 1 2 3 4M 4	AD------add doubles
5 + 6 a 5s pth	ca fco cah coh wo sc asc dk	0 1 2 3 4M 4	AD1-----add dbls +/-1
7 + 5 a 5s pth	ca fco cah coh wo sc asc dk	0 1 2 3 4M 4	AD2----add dbls +/-2
9 + 6 a 5s pth	ca fco cah coh wo sc asc dk	0 1 2 3 4M 4	AHF/C9-add higher facts use compensation w/9
8 + 4 a 5s pth	ca fco cah coh wo sc asc dk	0 1 2 3 4M 4	AHF/C7/8—add higher facts/use compensation with 7/8
7 + 8 a 5s pth	ca fco cah coh wo sc asc dk	0 1 2 3 4M 4	AHF/C7/8—add higher facts/use compensation with 7/8

Codes	**Types of Strategies**	**Strategy Levels**
a - automatic 5s - 5 seconds pth - prolonged thinking time	ca - counted all fco – finger counted on cah – counted all in head coh – counted on in head wo - wrong operation sc - self corrected asc - attempted to self-correct dk - didn't know	0 – doesn't know 1 – counting strategies by ones or skip counting using fingers, drawings or manipulatives 2 - mental math/solving in head 3 - using known facts and strategies 4M - automatic recall from memory 4 – automatic recall and students have number sense

Part 2: Flexibility/Efficiency

Teacher: We are now going to administer Part 2 of the Running Record. In this part of the Running Record we are going to talk about what strategies you use when you are solving basic addition facts. I am going to tell you a problem and then ask you to tell me how you think about it. I am also going to ask you about some different types of facts. Take your time as you answer and tell me what you are thinking as you see and do the math. I am going to take notes so I can remember everything that happened during this Running Record.

Add 0 0 + 1	Add 1 2 + 1	Add w/in 5 or 10 3 + 2 2 + 6	Add to Make 10 4 + 6
What happens when you add zero to a number? ___ same # ___other ___can't articulate	What strategy do you use when you add 1 to a number? ___ next counting # ___other ___can't articulate	How do you solve 4 + 0? And 6 + 3? ___ count on from big # __ other ___can't articulate	How do you solve 5 + 5? ___ count on from big # __ other ___can't articulate
What would be the answer to... 3 + 0 0 + 5 8 + 0	What would be the answer to.... 4 + 1 1 + 7 10 + 1	w/in 5 w/in 10 1 + 3 5 + 4 2 + 2 2 + 7	I'm going to give you a number and I want you to give me the number that makes 10 with it. If I give you 7, how many more to make 10? If I give you ____ how many more to 10? 9? 2? 6? 3?
Do they know this strategy? No/Emerging/Yes A0 Level 0 1 2 3 4M 4	Do they know this strategy? No/Emerging/Yes A1 Level 0 1 2 3 4M 4	Do they know this strategy? No/Emerging/Yes A10 Level 0 1 2 3 4M 4	Do they know this strategy? No/Emerging/Yes AM10 Level 0 1 2 3 4M 4
Add 10 10 + 4	**Doubles 7 + 7**	**Doubles +/- 1 5 + 6**	**Doubles +/- 2 7 + 5**
What strategy do you use when you add 10 to a number? ___ teen #s decompose to 10 and 1's ___other ___can't articulate	How would you solve 6 + 6? ___ doubles ___ other ___can't articulate	How would you solve 6 + 7? ___ doubles +/-1 ___ other ___can't articulate	If a friend did not know how to solve 7 + 9, what would you tell her to do? ___ doubles +/-2 ___other ___can't articulate
How would you solve ____? 10 + 2 10 + 6 10 + 8 Do they know this strategy?	How would you solve _____? 4 + 4 8 + 8 9 + 9 What kind of facts are these? _____ Do they know this strategy?	How would you solve ____? 2 + 3 3 + 4 8 + 9 Do they know this strategy?	How would you solve....? 2 + 4 8 + 6 9 + 11 Do they know this strategy?
No/Emerging/Yes A10 Level 0 1 2 3 4M 4	No/Emerging/Yes AD Level 0 1 2 3 4M 4	No/Emerging/Yes AD1 Level 0 1 2 3 4M 4	No/Emerging/Yes AD2 Level 0 1 2 3 4M 4

(Continued)

(Continued)

Bridge through 10 (9) 9 + 6	Bridge through 10 (7/8) 8 + 4	Part 3: Mathematical Disposition
If your friend was stuck solving 9 + 5, what would you tell him to do? ___ bridge 10 ___other ___can't articulate How do you solve _____? 9 + 3 9 + 6	What strategy would you use to solve 8 + 3? ___ bridge 10 ___other ___can't articulate How would you solve _____? 4 + 7? 8 + 5?	Do you like math? What do you find easy? What do you find tricky? What do you do when you get stuck?
Do they know this strategy? No/Emerging/Yes AHF/C9 Level 0 1 2 3 4M 4	Do they know this strategy? No/Emerging/Yes AHF/C 7/8 Level 0 1 2 3 4M 4	Question Prompts: That's interesting/fascinating: tell me what you did. That's interesting/fascinating: tell me how you solved it. That's interesting/fascinating: tell me what you were thinking. How did you solve this problem? Can you tell me more about how you solve these types of problems? What do you mean when you say _____? (i.e. ten friends/neighbor numbers etc.)

General Observations (to be filled out after the interview)

Instructional Response:
Fluency Focus areas (circle all that apply): flexibility   efficiency   accuracy   automaticity

What addition strategy should the instruction focus on?

A0 A1 Aw5 Aw10 AM10 A10 AD AD1 AD2 AHF/C9 AHF/C 7/8

For his/her current instructional level, what is the predominant way in which the student is arriving at the answers? 0 1 2 3 4M 4 _____

Overall, what is the way in which the students calculated the answers?: 0 1 2 3 4M 4

Comments/Notes about gestures, behaviors, remarks:

*In most states k fluency is within 5 and 1st grade fluency is within 10 and 2nd grade within 20. However, some states k is within 10 and 1st and 2nd is within 20.

Figure 2.2 Exit Slip Example

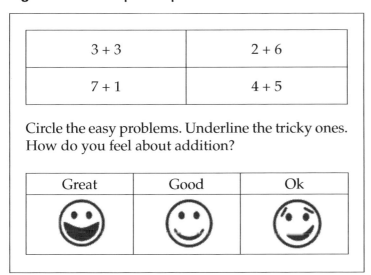

3 + 3	2 + 6
7 + 1	4 + 5

Circle the easy problems. Underline the tricky ones.
How do you feel about addition?

Great	Good	Ok
😃	🙂	🙂

Figure 2.3 Differentiated Practice

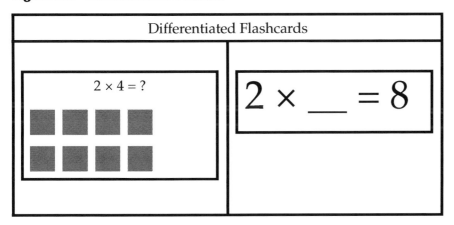

Differentiated Flashcards

2 × 4 = ?

$2 \times \underline{\hspace{1cm}} = 8$

students to make sure that they understand the math. For example, students might know the 8 multiplication facts by skip counting by 8's. So, they can get an answer but they don't have strategic competence. We want them to have flexibility and efficiency with numbers, for example in this case thinking about doubling 4's or another efficient strategy. We would practice it in a variety of ways with manipulatives, with sketches and with the numbers. We would also have the students verbalize what they are doing and contextualize it by telling stories (NCTM, 2014).

When we are thinking about grouping, it is about meeting the needs of the students where they are and taking them to what they need to learn at that grade level, so students are emerging in their learning along the continuum. It is about creating flexible groups that students can move through as they work on different concepts. These groups should never be "fixed" and track students throughout the year. They are temporary, flexible and focused groups that teach students what they need, when they need it and then students move on to different work (see Figures 2.3 and 2.4).

Figure 2.4 Types of Groups

Group 1: Emergent	Group 2: Early Fluent	Group 3: Fluent	Group 4: Advanced Fluent
These are the students who are working below grade level in some areas. They have many strengths but also they often have many gaps and misunderstandings. It is important to work on closing gaps as well as highly scaffolding (but not overscaffolding) current grade level material.	These students are approaching grade level. They know some stuff and they are shaky on other things. They have some gaps and need some remediation.	These students are right at grade level. Sometimes, these students have a limited understanding of the math. Oftentimes, they can get the answer but they have trouble explaining what they did and why they did it.	These students are working above grade level. This doesn't mean that the work should be done from the next grade level though, as Kathy Richardson notes it is important to go deeper with concepts rather than to jump to the next ones.
A student can be an emergent learner in one area and an advanced fluent learner in another. We shouldn't give students labels that stick with them all year. As Dr. Kim Reid always said, "Labels are for boxes." Although we need a way to describe how students are doing in particular areas, we must never categorize them with fixed labels.			
"Rather than viewing some children as 'low' or 'behind' or 'lacking in skills,' kidwatching teachers view all children as creative, capable learners – on their way to 'achieving control over the conventions of [math]- always "in process" always moving forward . . .' (Flukey, 1997, p. 219 cited in Owocki & Goodman, 2002)." Students move and develop along their own trajectory. With the appropriate scaffolding we can teach everybody and move them to achieving grade level standards.			

Rotations

Teachers can assign students where they are going to go, visiting different stations every day. Another way to do it is to give the student a menu for the week with Can Do's and Must Do's. Either way, students should do fluency, word problems, place value and work from the current unit of study.

Standards-Based

Every guided math lesson should be centered around priority/readiness/power standards. There are so many standards to teach, so we have to focus. We have to get in there, dig deep and discuss ideas so that students can learn them. When students sit down in the group, the first thing the teacher should talk about is the work they are going to be doing for the day. The *I can* or *I am* learning to statement should be up, and the students should discuss what they are going to be learning and what the criteria of success for that learning will look like. There is an ongoing discussion about whether to say *I can* or *I am* learning to. *I can* is more of a statement about what students will be able to do in the future. *I am* learning to speaks more to the continuum of learning and allows for students to be at different places along that continuum.

Dixon points out that, sometimes, we shouldn't tell the students the *I can* statement at the beginning all of the time because then you in essence tell the ending of the story before it begins (2018a). This is an excellent point; it depends on where you are at in the concept and skill cycle and what the lesson of the day is. If you are trying to get students to explore and wonder about something, then don't upfront it, but discuss it at the end after they have explored the topic. However, if you are working on something that you have been doing for a while, you can say, "Today we are going to continue looking at . . . "

Depth of Knowledge

Guided math lessons are about building Depth of Knowledge with students. They should reach a variety of levels, not just level one activities. For example, instead of just telling stories like: There were 3 boxes with 4 cupcakes in each box. How many cupcakes are there? Teachers should ask questions like: The answer is 12 cupcakes. What is the question? Instead of just asking *what is 3 × 2*, teachers should also say things like *give me two different ways to make 15*. We want students to be reasoning about numbers in a variety of ways, using as many scaffolds as they need to become confident and competent.

Scaffolding

Scaffolds are a fundamental part of guided math lessons. There are so many different types of scaffolds. We are going to discuss grouping scaffolds, language scaffolds and tool scaffolds. Grouping scaffolds help students to become proficient by having students work with partners and in small groups, before they practice the skill on their own. This is the social aspect of grappling with the content. Oftentimes, students learn a great deal from each other through discussions and interactions. In the group, you can partner the students up, watch them play the game, take notes and ask different questions to guide them as they work together.

Language is often scaffolded with illustrated pictures of the vocabulary and language stems on sentence strips. Dixon (2018b) talks about how in the beginning of learning about a concept it can be productive for students to have to explain the topic without the "cover" of the vocabulary. Meaning that sometimes students will use words but not understand the concepts, but their lack of understanding can be hidden by the use of the correct vocabulary. If they don't have that, then they have to explain the math. In later lessons, when students understand the math, then it's ok to upfront the vocabulary.

Scaffolding is so important and yet we have to be really careful not to overscaffold and as Dixon warns to also avoid "just in case" scaffolding (2018c). We want to help students as they need it, but we do not want to steal the struggle. Students need the opportunity to engage in the productive struggle, but it should not be an unproductive struggle (Hiebert & Grouws, 2007; Blackburn, 2018). There is a very careful balance act that teachers conduct when scaffolding in a guided math group.

In the guided math group, teachers should make sure that tools are part of the learning cycle. In planning to unpack the concepts and skills in small groups, teachers should think about the ways in which students can wrestle with topics concretely, pictorially and abstractly. There should also be an emphasis on verbalization and contextualization (NCTM, 2014). The magic of the manipulatives is the conversation and the activities that are done along with them. Students need to reflect on and explain the concepts and how the manipulatives are being used to model those concepts. In a small group, students should be doing the math and exploring and discussing the ideas as they use the manipulatives (Ball, 1992; Baroody, 1989; Bruner, 1960; Burns, n.d.)

Engagement

Engagement is important. Research links engagement to students' *affect*—their feelings and emotions about learning (Mcleod, 1992 cited in Ingram). We find that students' engagement is shaped around the sociocultural environment in which they are learning: how they are constructing knowledge together through discussions, activities and the norms of learning (Op 't Eynde, 2004; Boaler & Greeno, 2000; Greeno, Collins, & Resnick, 1996). The interactions that students have in small guided math groups are very important. They help to shape students' mathematical identities—who and what they see themselves as in terms of a mathematician.

We find that students are engaged when they participate in strong lessons in a strong community. A strong lesson has a clear purpose, is relevant and makes sense to their lives; it is brain-friendly and flows easily allowing them to quickly get into a "good 'work-flow,'" dive deep into the material (Claflin, 2014). The strong community of learners in essence means that "they got each other's back!" Everybody is in it to win it with each other. Students are helpful, trusting, risk-taking and comfortable. In the small group, they should be willing to try things out and assured that it is not always going to work the first time and that they might not get it even the second time around but that with perseverance they can learn it.

Another really important aspect of working with children is the wonder of learning. The guided math table is a special experience. I like to have guided math journals and special pencils and toolkits for students to work with at the table. Students look forward to coming to the guided math group. Often, I use dice, dominos, cards and board games. Since the same structure can be used, the students are ready to work on the content. Meaning, if we play bingo, then students know that structure, so they can immediately focus on the content. I might play a Multiply by 5's and 10's bingo game with one group and a Multiply by 2s, 4s and 8s bingo game with another group.

Student Accountability

While the students are working in math workstations, they should be filling out different sheets of the work they are doing (see Figures 2.5, 2.6 and 2.7). They should be recording what they are doing. Some sheets record everything that students are doing. Other games have students record only some of their work. The most important thing about math workshop is that you organize it well from the beginning. You must do the first 20 days. In the first 20 days you teach the students how to work in the workshop. Here is a resource for that: www.drnickinewton.com/downloads/.

Students have to learn how to work independently before you start pulling them in to guided math groups. The premise of Math Workshop is that all students can work on their own productively, before you start working with them in small groups.

There are two key elements to a good workstation. The first is a clear goal for the workstation. Students need to know what the math is and how they are going to work on that math and what it looks like when they are actually learning that math. The second is that they have an accountability system so that they know the teacher will be monitoring their work.

Figure 2.5 Example 1: Student Recording Sheet

Comparing Numbers with Fraction. Dice		
Roll the dice. Record your roll. Compare with the symbols. Whoever has the highest number wins a point. Whoever gets 5 points first wins the round. Whoever wins 3 rounds wins the game.		
Partner 1	**< = >**	**Partner 2**

Figure 2.6 Example 2: Student Recording Sheet

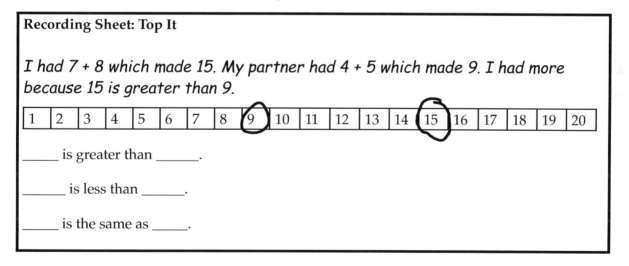

Recording Sheet: Top It

I had 7 + 8 which made 15. My partner had 4 + 5 which made 9. I had more because 15 is greater than 9.

| 1 | 2 | 3 | 4 | 5 | 6 | 7 | 8 | 9 | 10 | 11 | 12 | 13 | 14 | 15 | 16 | 17 | 18 | 19 | 20 |

_____ is greater than _____.

_____ is less than _____.

_____ is the same as _____.

Figure 2.7 Example 3: Student Recording Sheet

> **Recording Sheet: Board Game**
>
> *When I went around the board, I solved several multiplication fact problems. I used different strategies to help me.*
>
> I solved:
>
> $2 \times 2 = 4$
> $3 \times 5 = 15$
> $4 \times 6 = 24$

Key Points

- Assessment
- Grouping
- Differentiation
- Rotations
- Standards-based
- Depth of Knowledge
- Scaffolding
- Engagement
- Student accountability

Chapter Summary

The key to great guided math groups is assessment. When you have great assessments, then you can group appropriately for differentiation that matters. Lessons should be standards-based. Teachers must always plan for the level of rigor in the lesson. Lessons should be scaffolded with language supports, tools, templates and student grouping. All the other students must be accountable to the work they are doing in the workstations. Engagement is necessary.

Reflection Questions

1. What specific assessments do you have around the priority standards?
2. In what ways are you evaluating your lessons for rigor?
3. In what ways are you scaffolding lessons?
4. How do you know that the other students are on task and learning in the math workstations?

References

Ball, D. L. (1992). Magical hopes: Manipulatives and the reform of math education. *American Educator: The Professional Journal of the American Federation of Teachers, 16*(2), 14–18, 46–47.

Baroody, A. J. (1989). Manipulatives don't come with guarantees. *Arithmetic Teacher, 37*(2), 4–5.

Blackburn, B. (2018). Retrieved January 5, 2020 from www.ascd.org/ascd-express/vol14/num11/productive-struggle-is-a-learners-sweet-spot.aspx

Boaler, J., & Greeno, J. G. (2000). Identity, agency, and knowing in mathematical worlds. In J. Boaler (Ed.), *Multiple perspectives on mathematics teaching and learning* (pp. 171–200). Westport, CT: Ablex Publishing.

Bruner, J. S. (1960). On learning mathematics. *The Mathematics Teacher, 53*(8), 610–619.

Burns, M. (n.d.). *How to make the most of manipulatives.* Retrieved August 28, 2016 from http://teacher.scholastic.com/lessonrepro/lessonplans/instructor/burns.htm?nt_id=4&url=http://store.scholastic.com/Books/Hardcovers/Harry-Potter-and-the-Chamber-of-SecretsThe-Illustrated-Edition-Book-2?eml=SSO/aff/20160429/21181/banner/EE/affiliate/////2-247765/&affiliate_id=21181&click_id=1707726852

Claflin, P. (2014). Retrieved January 20, 2020 from www.theanswerisyes.org/2014/12/08/student-engagement-checklist/

Dixon. (2018a). Retrieved January 4, 2020 from www.dnamath.com/blog-post/five-ways-we-undermine-efforts-to-increase-student-achievement-and-what-to-do-about-it/

Dixon. (2018b). Retrieved January 4, 2020 from www.dnamath.com/blog-post/five-ways-we-undermine-efforts-to-increase-student-achievement-and-what-to-do-about-it-part-4-of-5/

Dixon. (2018c). Retrieved January 4, 2020 from www.dnamath.com/blog-post/five-ways-we-undermine-efforts-to-increase-student-achievement-and-what-to-do-about-it-part-3-of-5/

Greeno, J. G., Collins, A. M., & Resnick, L. B. (1996). Cognition and learning. In D. C. Berliner & R. C. Calfee (Eds.), *Handbook of educational psychology* (pp. 15–46). London: Prentice Hall International.

Hiebert, J., & Grouws, D. A. (2007). The effects of classroom mathematics teaching on students' learning. In F. K. Lester Jr. (Ed.), *Second handbook of research on mathematics teaching and learning* (pp. 371–404). Charlotte, NC: Information Age.

McLeod, D. B. (1992). Research on affect in mathematics education: A reconceptualization. In D. Grouws (Ed.), *Handbook of research on mathematics teaching and learning* (pp. 575–596). New York: NCTM and Macmillan.

National Council of Teachers of Mathematics. (2014). *Principles to actions: Ensuring mathematical success for all.* Reston, VA: National Council of Teachers of Mathematics.

Op 't Eynde, P. (2004). A socio-constructivist perspective on the study of affect in mathematics education. In M. J. Hoines & A. B. Fuglestad (Eds.), *28th conference of the international group for the psychology of mathematics education* (Vol. 1, pp. 118–122). Bergen, Norway: Bergen University College.

Owocki, G., & Goodman, Y. M. (2002). *Kidwatching: Documenting children's literacy development.* Portsmouth, NH: Heinemann.

Richardson, K. (n.d.). Retrieved January 17, 2020 from http://assessingmathconcepts.com/

Shafer, L. (2016). *Summer math loss. Why kids lose math knowledge, and how families can work to counteract it.* Retrieved January 15, 2019 from www.gse.harvard.edu/news/uk/16/06/summer-math-loss

3

Architecture of a Small Group Lesson

Guided math groups can look many different ways. Sometimes they are more of an exploration of a concept with manipulatives like 1-inch tiles and counters; other times they are practicing a skill in the form of a dice game. The elements of the guided math lesson are the same, but the sequencing can be different. For example, you might start with an energizer and then review a skill and play a game to practice that skill. On the other hand, you might be exploring multiplication of a number with Cuisenaire rods first and then afterwards discuss more in depth what the math you were exploring was about.

Oftentimes, a small group lesson will begin with an introduction to the lesson. In this introduction, students could go over the agenda. The teacher can write it up as an agenda so students know what the general outline of the lesson is and what they will be doing. At some point in the lesson, depending on the type of lesson, the teacher would then go over the "*I am learning to*" statement as well as what it looks like when students can actually do that skill or understand that concept (success criteria).

At some point in the lesson, there should be a discussion about the math vocabulary and phrases that are associated with the current topic, if they are already familiar with the words. Dixon points out that we should discuss the vocabulary at the end of the lesson sometimes, because it can mask understanding. Meaning that students can be using the vocabulary but not really understanding what it means (see Dixon, 2018, blog4). It is good to have students stretch their thinking and find the words to describe what they are doing and then later name it with math words.

There are many ways to begin lessons. They can begin with either a discussion, an exploration or an activity. The teacher might model it or might just jump into the topic. Oftentimes, the teacher will ask the students to give their input about the topic before they begin. After a time of exploration, the students will begin to further explore the topic, either on their own, with a partner or with the whole small group.

At the end, the teacher will lead the debrief. This is where the students will discuss what the math was for the day, as well as how they practiced that math. They should also talk about how they feel they are doing with that math. This is the part of the lesson where students are reflecting and monitoring their process. They talk about the parts of the topic that are "easy-peasy" and the parts that are "tricky." Language is important, so instead of saying difficult or hard, I tend to say "tricky, fuzzy or climbing." Using a mountain metaphor can help students explain their journey. I explain to students that they could be just looking at the mountain from the base, climbing but not at the top yet, almost at the top or at the top (whereby they can say *it's sunny on the summit*).

Planning

Planning is key (see Figures 3.1 through 3.6). As you are planning for the guided math lesson, it is important to think about the differences between the content, the context and the activity. The content could be to teach students how to compare fractions. The context could be a story about

DOI: 10.4324/9781003169543-3

Figure 3.1 I can chart

I am going to *play a multiplication game.*
So that I can *practice the 5 and 10 facts.*
I will know that I can do it when I can *multiply by 5s and 10s using models and/or mental math.*

comparing fractions in real life. The activity could be to play a card game where they have to compare fractions using visual scaffolds. This comes up when mapping math content. There is a difference between an activity and a skill. An activity is to actually do something, like play a board game. The skill is the verb—to be able to compare a fraction. The teacher should be planning success criteria for both the product and the process. An example of content criteria (see Figure 3.1):

An example of process criteria is to think about what practices you want students to be able to do:

♦ I can *explain* how to multiply by 5 using different strategies.
♦ I can *model* multiplying by 5 in different ways.

Clarke states that when we define process success criteria for students, it helps them do these six things:

1. Ensure appropriate focus
2. Provide opportunity to clarify their understanding
3. Identify success for themselves
4. Begin to identify where the difficulties lie
5. Discuss how they will improve
6. Monitor their own progress

(cited in Dyer, n.d.)

In the guided math group, everyone should know what the criteria is and should discuss it. Dyer notes that it is important for students to think about the "How will we know?" question. When students wrestle with this question they begin "to understand the learning behind the learning target."

> This enables students to better understand what teachers expect them to know, understand, or be able to do, as well as what constitutes a proficient performance. This allows students to support each other and take responsibility for their own learning by helping them accurately and appropriately evaluate learning against shared expectations and make any necessary adjustments to the learning. Students become activated as learners.
>
> (n.d.)

Think about this in terms of your guided math lessons. Do the students understand the success criteria? Do they know what they are expected to know, understand and be able to do? What are you looking for in the products or performances to know that the students were successful? How will you judge if it was successful? What will you use to judge the effectiveness of the product or performance? What counts as successful?

If the objective is for students to learn different efficient and flexible strategies for adding, then the success criteria might be that:

♦ Students' explanations include the names of the strategies
♦ Students can discuss different ways to think about the same problem
♦ In the explanations, students include a clear description of what they did (they can verbalize the strategy)
♦ Students can model their thinking

You could also have this discussion at the end of the lesson, after students have explored many different strategies. You could then talk about what it means to be flexible and efficient. You could have a checklist or rubric that has the criteria on it.

In the guided math group, the goal is for both teacher and students to be questioning. The expected answers should require thinking, not just a quick yes or no. Students should be thinking and explaining the work. Guided math should not be show and tell. It should be teachers springboarding students into mathematical thinking. The guided math group is a space for the "having of a very good idea" by all. In the guided math group the students should be taking the responsibility for learning and reflecting on their learning, as well as evaluating themselves and others. They should not be passive listeners or just "yes men and women." They should be active participants in the construction of rich mathematical ideas. To make this happen, there must be a great deal of planning.

More Planning

In the guided math group, there can be an agenda (Figure 3.2). Whether or not you make it public, the teacher should have an idea of the structure of the lesson. I usually make it public.

Planning and Preparation

There are many different planning templates, but they basically all have the same information. When planning it is important to think about the big idea, the enduring understanding, the essential question, the *I am* learning to statement, the assessments and possibly on the same template or a different one, the workstations or menu activities. See the list of the templates below (Figures 3.3–3.11).

Figure 3.2 Agenda

Introduction

Agenda

♦ *I am* learning to/*I can*
♦ Vocabulary/language frames
♦ Launch by teacher
♦ Student activity (alone/pairs/group)
♦ Wrap-up/reflection
♦ Next steps

Figure 3.3 Quick Plan

Week:	Assessments	Workstations
Big Idea:	Entrance Slips:	Group 1
Enduring Understanding:	Exit Slips:	Group 2
Essential Question		Group 3
I am learning to . . .		Group 4

Figure 3.4 Guided Math Planning Template 1

Unit of Study: Big Idea: Enduring Understanding: Standard:			Essential Question: Vocabulary: Language Frame: I Can Statement:	
	Group 1:	Group 2:	Group 3:	Group 4:
Monday	Lesson: Materials: DOK Level: Concrete/ Pictorial/Abstract	Lesson: Materials: DOK Level: Concrete/Pictorial/Abstract	Lesson: Materials: DOK Level: Concrete/ Pictorial/Abstract	Lesson: Materials: DOK Level: Concrete/ Pictorial/Abstract
Tuesday	Lesson: Materials: DOK Level: Concrete/ Pictorial/Abstract	Lesson: Materials: DOK Level: Concrete/Pictorial/Abstract	Lesson: Materials: DOK Level: Concrete/ Pictorial/Abstract	Lesson: Materials: DOK Level: Concrete/ Pictorial/Abstract
Wednesday	Lesson: Materials: DOK Level: Concrete/ Pictorial/Abstract	Lesson: Materials: DOK Level: Concrete/Pictorial/Abstract	Lesson: Materials: DOK Level: Concrete/ Pictorial/Abstract	Lesson: Materials: DOK Level: Concrete/ Pictorial/Abstract
Thursday	Lesson: Materials: DOK Level: Concrete/ Pictorial/Abstract	Lesson: Materials: DOK Level: Concrete/Pictorial/Abstract	Lesson: Materials: DOK Level: Concrete/ Pictorial/Abstract	Lesson: Materials: DOK Level: Concrete/ Pictorial/Abstract
Friday	Lesson: Materials: DOK Level: Concrete/ Pictorial/Abstract	Lesson: Materials: DOK Level: Concrete/Pictorial/Abstract	Lesson: Materials: DOK Level: Concrete/ Pictorial/Abstract	Lesson: Materials: DOK Level: Concrete/ Pictorial/Abstract

Figure 3.5 Guided Math Planning Template 2

Guided Math Groups	
Big Ideas: **Enduring Understandings:** **Essential Questions:** **Vocabulary:** **Language Frames:**	**Cycle of Engagement: Concrete, Pictorial, Abstract** **Depth of Knowledge Level:** **1 2 3 4** **Standard/I can statement:**
Group 1: Novice Students:	Group 2: Apprentice Students:
Group 3: Practitioner Students:	Group 4: Expert Students:

Figure 3.6 Guided Math Planning Template 3

Guided Math Lesson Plan: Group:		
Week: Big Idea: Enduring Understanding:	Standard: I can/I am learning to statement:	Vocabulary: Language Frame: Materials:
Lesson: Intro: Guided Practice: Individual Practice: Sharing: Debrief:		
Comments/Notes: Next Steps:		

Figure 3.7 Guided Math Planning Template 4

Guided Math Lesson		
Big Ideas: Enduring Understandings: Essential Questions:	Vocabulary: Language Frame:	Standard: I can/I am learning to . . . Concrete/Pictorial/Abstract
DOK Level: 1 2 3 4	Goal: • Remediate • Teach • Dive Deeper	Materials/Tools
		dice / board games / unifix cubes/bears/tiles
		dominos / counters / base ten blocks
		deck of cards / calculators / pattern blocks
		white boards/markers / gm journals / geoboards
Beginning of the Lesson	Guided Practice	Independent Practice
Assessment/Exit Slip	Discussion	Questions
Comments/Notes: Aha's: Wow: Rethink: Next Moves:		

Figure 3.8 Guided Math Planning Template 5

Guided Math		
Group: **Week:**		
Big Idea: Enduring Understandings: Essential Questions:	Vocabulary: Language Frame: DOK Level: 1 2 3 4	Lessons: 1st 2nd 3rd
Content Questions:		
Name	What I noticed	Next Steps

Figure 3.9 Guided Math Template 6

Topic:	
Big Idea: **Enduring Understanding:** **Essential Question:** **I can statement:**	**Materials**
Cycle of Engagement **Concrete:** **Pictorial:** Abstract	**Vocabulary and Language Frames** Vocabulary: Talk Frame:
	Other notes:

Figure 3.10 Differentiation Template

Three Differentiated Lessons		
Emerging	On Grade Level	Above Grade Level

WATCH OUT
Misunderstandings and Misconceptions

Figure 3.10a Differentiated Planning Template

Group 1: Emergent	Group 2: Early Fluent	Group 3: Fluent	Group 4: Advanced Fluent

WATCH OUT Misunderstandings and Misconceptions

Figure 3.11 Guided Math Extended Planning Template

Guided Math Planning Sheet	
Launch	
Model	
Checking for Understanding	
Guided Practice/ Checking for Understanding	
Set Up for Independent Practice	

Key Points

♦ Components of a Small Group Lesson

  ○ I am learning to/I can
  ○ Vocabulary/language frames
  ○ Launch by teacher
  ○ Student activity (alone/pairs/group)
  ○ Wrap-up
  ○ Next steps

♦ Planning template
♦ Discussion throughout

Chapter Summary

There are many different ways to do small guided math groups. Teachers must plan for the learning goal, the vocabulary supports, the tools, the launch of the lesson, the students practicing the math, the wrap-up, the reflection and the next steps. All of these elements are an important part of the lesson. They all contribute to the success of the guided math group. Using planning templates with these elements on them helps teachers to plan for each of the elements.

Reflection Questions

1. Do your guided math lessons have all of the elements in them?
2. What types of templates are you currently using for guided math groups?
3. What is an element that you need to focus on in the architecture?

References

Dixon, J. (2018). *Small Group Instruction {from the (Un)Productive Practices Series}*. Five Ways We Undermine Efforts to Increase Student Achievement (and what to do about it). Blog Post 4: www.dnamath.com/blog-post/five-ways-we-undermine-efforts-to-increase-student-achievement-and-what-to-do-about-it-part-4-of-5/

Dyer, K. (n.d.). Retrieved January 20, 2020 from www.nwea.org/blog/2018/what-you-need-to-know-when-establishing-success-criteria-in-the-classroom/

4

Talk in the Guided Math Group

One of the most important things that happen in the guided math group is the discussion. We have to teach students to be active participants and engaged listeners. We want them to respect each other deeply and seek to truly understand each other without judgement. They have to learn to develop and defend their thinking, justify their answers and respectfully disagree with each other. The National Council of Teachers of Mathematics (NCTM) defines math talk as "the ways of representing, thinking, talking, and agreeing and disagreeing that teachers and students use to engage in [mathematical] tasks" (NCTM, 1991).

Questions

It is so important to ask good questions. The questions should reach beyond the answer. As Phil Daro notes, we have to go "beyond answer-getting" (https://vimeo.com/79916037). The questions in the guided math group should be designed to get students to understand more fundamentally the mathematics of the grade level. Good questions don't just happen, they are planned for. The teacher should know ahead of time the types of questions that she will ask and why she will ask them. In the plan for the lesson, the teacher should brainstorm some possible questions that push student thinking. These are not yes or no questions, but rather ones that require students to explain themselves, show what they know and defend and justify their thinking (see Figure 4.1).

When students are sitting in that group, they should be having an engaging experience that builds mathematical knowledge and skills. At the table, students should be encouraged to actively participate. They should be thinking out loud, sharing their thoughts, respectively analyzing and critiquing the thoughts and actions of others and taking risks throughout the explorations. We should always be thinking about the levels of rigor of the conversation that the students are engaged in (see Figure 4.2).

It is very important to include *Open Questions* as part of your repertoire at the guided math table. Here is an example: *The answer is 12 elephants. What is the question?* Although you will ask some questions that require students to remember a fact or show you that they can do a skill, your questions must extend beyond this level. You should be focusing on questions that have more than one answer or way of solving the problem.

Questions That Pique Curiosity

Your questions should pique curiosity. They should lead students into further explorations. They don't have to be answered immediately. Students should have a sense of wonder. There should be some "Aha" moments, some "Wow" moments and some "I don't get it" moments.

For example, "What if we didn't have addition?" "Tell me 3 situations in which you would use subtraction." "Why is multiplication important in real life?"

DOI: 10.4324/9781003169543-4

Figure 4.1 Planning for Great Questions

Before the Lesson	During the Lesson	After the Lesson
Plan what you want to get your students to think about. The tasks that we choose will determine the thinking that occurs.	**Observe, monitor and note what is happening in the group. Checklists, Post-its and anecdotal note structures work well here.**	**Reflect, assess and decide what's next.**
How will you go about that? What questions will you ask them?	What is your data collection system during the lesson?	What did you see?
		What did you hear?
How will you set them up to actively listen and productively participate?	How will you scaffold student questioning?	What did the students do?
How will you get them to engage with the ideas of others?	How will you scaffold student to student interactions?	What do you need to do next?
		What instructional moves will you make?
How will you get them to offer detailed explanations of their own thinking using numbers, words and models?		What pedagogical moves will you make?
Plan for misconceptions. How will you address them and redirect students?		

Figure 4.2 Planning for Great Questions

In terms of rigor there are four levels of questions.

DOK 1	DOK 2 **At this level students explain their thinking.**	DOK 3 **At this level students have to justify, defend and prove their thinking with objects, drawings and diagrams.**
What is the answer to . . . ??? Can you model the problem? Can you identify the answer that matches this equation?	How do you know that the equation is correct? Can you pick the correct answer and explain why it is correct? Is there more than one answer? How can you model that problem in more than one way? What is another way to model that problem? Can you model that on the . . . ??? Give me an example of a . . . type of problem . . . Which answer is incorrect? Explain your thinking.	Can you prove that your answer is correct? Prove that . . . Explain why that is the answer . . . . Show me how to solve that and explain what you are doing.

* Level 4 is more strategic project-based thinking questions.

Student to Student Conversations

It is crucial that the teacher sets up a discussion where students are asking each other questions. They could have question rings, bookmarks, mini-anchor charts or other scaffolds to help them ask each other questions (see Figures 4.3–4.5). In these conversations one of the things that students are doing is listening to each other and comparing what they did.

Probing Questions

Teacher questions as well as student to student questions should provide insight into student thinking. During the guided math lesson and after it, the teacher should jot down what they have learned about student thinking, student knowledge and how they are making sense of the math they are learning.

Figure 4.3 Question Bookmark

Question Bookmark
Questions we could ask each other.   How do you know?   Are you sure about that?   What is another way to do that?   Why did you use that model?   Can you explain your thinking?

Figure 4.4 Talk Cards/Talk Ring

I agree because...	I disagree because..	I need some time to think.	Why is that true?

Are you sure?	Do you agree or disagree?	Can you think of another way?	I'm confused still..
Yes I'm sure because No, I'm not sure. I'm thinking about it.	or	Way 1 Way 2	

Figure 4.5 5 Talk Moves Poster

5 talk moves poster				
Revoice	Restate	Reason	Wait Time	Group participation
I heard you say...	*Who can say what she said in your own words?*	*Are you sure? Can you prove it?*	*Give me a few seconds*	*Who wants to add to that?*

Scaffolding Questions for ELLs

Students should understand the questions being asked. The language should be accessible, and everyone should have a way to enter the conversation. When thinking about instruction with English Language Learners, we must consider the type of language support they will need (https://mathsolutions.com/math-talk/; http://fspsscience.pbworks.com/w/file/fetch/80214878/Leveled_20Questions_20for_20ELLs; www.aworldoflanguagelearners.com/asking-answering-questions-with-ells/). Oftentimes, they will need help with syntax and sentence structure so it is important to scaffold these into the conversation. Give students an opportunity to refer to language stems, use language bookmarks, write down and/or draw the answer (see Figure 4.6).

Although these are structures for ELLs, they are great question types to consider with the various students you are working with. They are also great ways to think about scaffolding questions for special education students.

Figure 4.6 Supporting English as an Additional Language Learners

Low levels of support: (advanced language learners) (levels 3 and 4)	Moderate levels of support: (developing language learners) (level 2)	High levels of support: (emerging language learners) (level 1)
Use a word bank (illustrated)	Use a sentence frame	Allow students to draw/write the answer
Explain how s/he did that.	I got the answer by _____.	Point to the . . .
Explain your thinking.	How can you use ____ to help you solve _____?	Show me your answer . . .
Explain your model/strategy.	How can you model that?	Which is the best answer?
What are two ways you could model your thinking?	What is the name of that strategy? (mini-anchor chart)	What is the name of that strategy? Do you see it here? (mini-anchor chart of strategies)
Can you describe your thinking?	How did you do that?	Give students a model sentence and a sentence frame
Can you show us what you did?	Why did you use that model/strategy?	
Can you describe how you did it?	How did s/he do that?	How did you get the answer?
Can you explain what s/he did?	Is it this or that?	How did you _____?
Why is that true?	Which strategy did you use? (visual support)	Do you agree? Yes or no?
Why is that not true?		Show me the _____
Explain how you did it.		Point to the _____
Decide if s/he is correct.		Circle the ____
		Can you point to the strategy you used?

Adapted from http://fspsscience.pbworks.com/w/file/fetch/80214878/Leveled_20Questions_20for_20ELLs www.aworldoflanguagelearners.com/asking-answering-questions-with-ells/

5 Talk Moves and More

The idea of having a framework for how students engage with each other is very important. Chapin, O'Connor, and Anderson (2009) theorized this framework around 5 talk moves: revoicing, restating, wait time, group participation and reasoning. There are also other really helpful frameworks (Kazem & Hintz, 2014; O'Connell & O'Connor, 2007). In the section that follows we will explore how some of these can help us structure the discussions in guided math groups. Oftentimes, these structures are used together; for example, a teacher might ask someone to restate what someone said and then encourage the group to add on (see Figures 4.7–4.16).

Figure 4.7 Revoicing

Revoicing		
What it is . . .	**What it does**	**What it sounds like**
The teacher restates in the words of the student what they just said.	This allows the student to hear back what they said, the other students to hear and process what has been said and everyone to think about it and make sure they understand it. This teaches students the power of hearing what they have said and trying to make sense of it.	*So you said . . . Is that correct?* *Let me make sure I understand, you are saying . . .* *So first you . . . and then you . . .* *So you used this model?* *So you used this strategy?*

Figure 4.8 Restating

Restating		
What it is . . .	**What it does**	**What it sounds like**
The teacher or other students restate in their own words what has been said. Then, they verify that restating with the original student.	This allows the student to hear back what they said, the other students to hear and process what has been said and everyone to think about it and make sure they understand it. This requires that students listen and pay attention to each other so they can restate what has been said. This teaches students how to listen to each other and make sense of what their peers are saying.	*Who can restate what Susie just said?* *Who can tell in their own words what Jamal just said?* *Who can explain what Carol meant when she said . . . ?*

Figure 4.9 Wait Time

Wait Time		
What it is . . .	**What it does**	**What it sounds like**
Teachers and students give each other 20–30 seconds of uninterrupted time to think, write or draw about what they are doing. This is done after the question is asked and then also when the answer is given. Students should be given the time to think about the answer and then respond to it.	This allows students the time to gather their thoughts, clarify their thinking for themselves and just time to think. It gives more people time to process what is happening. It teaches them the power of stopping to think instead of rushing into a conversation.	*Ok, now I am going to ask some questions, but I want you to take some think time before you answer.* *Terri just gave an answer. Let's think about what she just said before we respond.* *Show me with a silent hand signal when you are ready.* *Let's give everyone some time to think about this . . .* *Is everybody ready to share or do you need more time? Show me with a hand signal . . .*

Figure 4.10 Reasoning

Reasoning		
What it is . . .	**What it does**	**What it sounds like**
Teachers and students are asking each other for evidence and proof to defend and justify what they are saying.	This requires students to engage with each other's thinking. They must compare, contrast, justify and defend their thinking with the other group members. This teaches students the power of defending and justifying their thinking with evidence and proof.	*Why did you do that?* *Is that true?* *Why did you use that strategy?* *Can you prove it?* *Are you sure?* *How do you know?* *Why did you use that model?* *Does that make sense?* *Do you agree or disagree, and why or why not?* *How is your thinking like Tom's?* *Is there another way?*

Figure 4.11 Group Participation

Group Participation		
What it is . . .	**What it does**	**What it sounds like**
Students write down or model their thinking and then share it with the whole group.	This allows students to focus on their own strategies and models, jot them down and then share them. This teaches students the power of justifying and defending their thinking.	*Use a model to show . . .* *Illustrate your strategy.* *On your white boards, show us . . .* *In your guided math journal, show your thinking with numbers, words or pictures . . . be ready to share it with the group . . .*

Figure 4.12 Making Connections

To Make Connections		
What it is . . .	**What it does**	**What it sounds like**
Teachers and students are asking each other to make connections with what has been said at the table.	It requires students to listen to each other and think about how what they did connects to what someone else did. This teaches students the power of making connections with each other's thinking.	*How is that the same as what Marta did?* *How is that different from what Joe did?* *This is like what Trini did.* *How are these models the same and how are they different?* *How are these strategies the same and how are they different?*

Figure 4.13 Partner Talk

Partner Talk		
What it is . . .	**What it does**	**What it sounds like**
Students talk with their math partners about the math before they share out with the group. They might even draw or write something to share out.	This allows students to think out the math with each other, try to make sense of it and then be able to explain it to the whole group. This teaches students the power of working together to make sense of the math.	*Turn and talk to your partner.* *Tell your partner what you think and why you think that.* *Show and explain to your partner what you did.* *Defend your thinking to your partner.*

Figure 4.14 Student Participation

Prompting for Student Participation		
What it is . . .	**What it does**	**What it sounds like**
The teacher or the students encourage each other to participate in the conversation.	This allows students to participate with each other in the discussion. It openly asks for participation that builds on what has just been said. This teaches students the power of participating in a discussion.	*Who would like to add to that?* *Who wants to say more?* *How is what you did the same or different from the way Hong did it?* *Is there another model?* *Is there another strategy?* *Is there another way?*

Figure 4.15 Clarifying One's Own Thinking

Clarifying One's Own Thinking		
What it is . . .	**What it does**	**What it sounds like**
Teachers and students take the time to clarify their thinking.	It allows students to expand on their original thoughts. It requires them to give more examples, show more models and explain at a deeper level.	*Can you explain that further?* *Can you tell us more?* *What does that mean?* *Can you show us a model and explain it?* *Can you illustrate your strategy and explain it?*

Figure 4.16 Reflecting/Revising/Probing

Reflecting/Revising/Probing		
What it is . . .	**What it does**	**What it sounds like**
The teacher and the students take time to reflect on what has been said and possibly revise their thinking.	This gives students an opportunity to rethink about what they have just done. They get permission to change their minds. It teaches them the power of reflecting and revising their work.	*Did anybody change their mind?* *Did anybody revise their thinking?* *Now that you see this model, what do you think?* *Now that you see this strategy, what do you think?* *Thinking about what Jamal just said, how does that help us with our thinking?*

It is very important to use different talk moves and structures with students during guided math group in order to scaffold the discussions. The preceding structures can definitely get you started doing this. It is important to plan for what you want to work on so that it isn't just random conversations. You should be explicit with students when teaching these structures. For example, you might say, "Today we are working on wait time. I want you to think about giving each other the time to think as we talk. Remember, just because you are ready, doesn't mean your neighbor is yet."

Key Points

♦ Questions matter
♦ Plan for great questions
♦ DOK questions
♦ Questions that pique curiosity
♦ Student to student conversations
♦ Scaffolding questions for ELLs
♦ 5 talk moves and more

Chapter Summary

We must plan for good conversations. Planning matters. We must think about the ways in which we want our students to engage with each other and then actively do that in our groups. Think about the level of rigor of questions. Think about what kinds of questions pique curiosity. Consider how we get students to engage with each other respectfully, confidently and competently. We must stay conscious of scaffolding our questions for ELLs so that everyone has a way to enter the conversations. We need to consider the different types of talk moves that allow us to have rigorous, engaging and productive conversations.

Reflection Questions

1. What stands out for you in this chapter?
2. What will you enact right away?
3. What questions do you still have?

References

Chapin, S., O'Connor, C., & Anderson, N. (2009). *Classroom discussions: Using math talk to help students learn, Grades K-6* (2nd ed.). Sausalito, CA: Math Solutions Publications.

Daro, P. Retrieved December 11, 2020 from https://vimeo.com/79916037

Kazemi, E., & Hintz, A. (2014). *Intentional talk: How to structure and lead productive mathematical discussions.* Portland, ME: Stenhouse.

NCTM. (1991). *Professional standards for teaching mathematics.* Reston, VA: NCTM.

O'Connell, S., & O'Connor, K. (2007). *Introduction to communication, grades 3–5.* Heinemann.

Retrieved November 24, 2020 from http://fspsscience.pbworks.com/w/file/fetch/80214878/Leveled_20Questions_20for_20ELLs

Retrieved November 24, 2020 from https://mathsolutions.com/math-talk/

Retrieved November 24, 2020 from www.aworldoflanguagelearners.com/asking-answering-questions-with-ells/

5

Fluency

Basic fact fluency is a major part of third grade. Students should come into the grade having fluency with basic addition and subtraction facts as well as fluency with adding and subtracting 2-digit numbers. However, often times, these facts need to be reviewed and firmed up, and with special emphasis on learning the other higher fact strategies, such as doubles, doubles plus 1 and 2, bridging ten, half facts and higher addition and subtraction facts. Third graders are also expected to learn the multiplication and division facts within 100. Research says that we should devote at least 10 minutes a day to fluency practice (NCEE, 2009). It should be done as energizers and routines, in workstations and sometimes as guided math lessons. Teachers should integrate fluency work throughout the year because students learn their basic facts at different times.

Fluency is a multi-dimensional concept. We like to think of it as a four-legged stool: accuracy, flexibility, efficiency and instant recall (Brownell & Chazal, 1935; Brownell, 1956/1987; Kilpatrick, Swafford, & Findell, 2001; National Council of Teachers of Mathematics, 2000). Although we eventually want students to have instant recall, we need them to understand what they are doing with the numbers first. The emphasis in the guided math group is to do a variety of engaging, interactive, rigorous and student-friendly activities that build a fundamental understanding of how numbers are in relationship with each other. As you explore the facts with the students, be sure to do concrete, pictorial and abstract activities with them. There should be several ways for students to practice that are fun and challenging. Students should keep track of how they are doing as well.

    DOI: 10.4324/9781003169543-5

Research Note

- There has been a long debate on traditional fact-based instruction centered around memorization and strategy-based instruction centered around number sense and using strategies. Strategy-based instruction helps students to understand the math they are doing and to do it with eventual flexibility, efficiency, automaticity and accuracy (Baroody, Purpura, Eiland, Reid, & Paliwal, 2016; Henry & Brown, 2008; Thornton, 1978).
- Boaler (2015) argues that the emphasis of rote memorization through repetition and timed testing is "unnecessary and damaging."
- Several scholars have promoted engaging practice through strategy-based games and activities that can scaffold learning of basic facts (Van de Walle, 2007; Godfrey & Stone, 2013; Bay-Williams & Kling, 2019; Newton, 2016; Newton, Record, & Mello, 2020).

In this chapter we explore:

- Building arrays
- Division math mats
- Missing numbers
- Distributive property (splitting arrays) (see Figures 5.1 to 5.64)

Overview

Figure 5.1 Overview

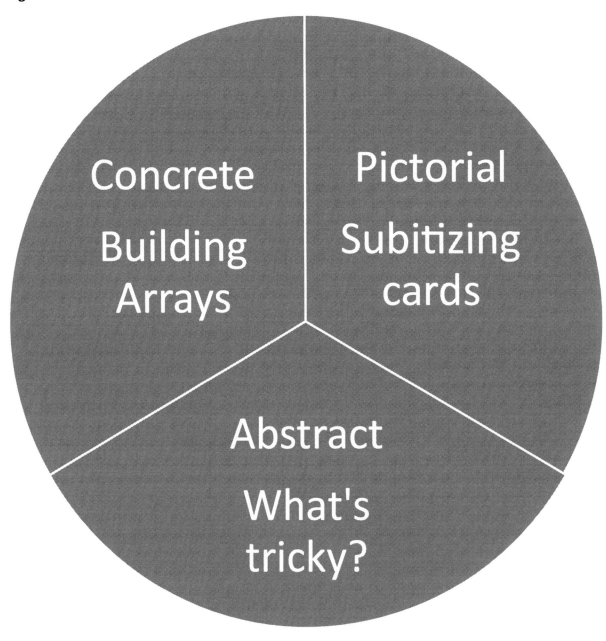

Figure 5.2 Planning Template

Building Arrays

Big Idea: Numbers, Operation Meanings & Relationships; Properties, Basic Facts & Algorithms **Enduring Understanding:** Students will understand that arrays are a representation of multiplication. **Essential Question:** Why are arrays important? How do we use them in real life? **I can statement:** I can represent basic multiplication facts with arrays.	**Materials** • Tools: counters (tiles, cubes, circles)

Cycle of Engagement	Vocabulary & Language Frames
Concrete:  **Pictorial:** **Abstract:** 2 groups of 3 2 × 3	**Vocabulary:** factors, array, product, row, column, horizontal, vertical, equal groups **Math Talk:** They array is ___ by ____. There are ___ columns and ____ rows. **Math Processes/Practices** • Problem Solving • Reasoning • Models • Tools • Precision • Structure • Pattern

Figure 5.3 Differentiated Lessons

Three Differentiated Lessons
In this series of lessons, students are working on building arrays. They are developing this concept through concrete activities, pictorial activities and abstract activities. Here are some things to think about as you do these lessons.

Emerging	On Grade Level	Above Grade Level
Do a lot of work with students building arrays with manipulatives. Remember this was introduced in second grade, up to 5 by 5 arrays. Also, students worked with the concept of repeated addition.	In third grade you are now building on the idea of arrays and the idea of multiplication. You will also work with the commutative, associative and distributive property.	If students have a thorough understanding of all of their facts within 100, then you can start exploring the 11's and 12's.

 Looking for Misunderstandings and Common Errors

Arrays are often easy for students to understand.

Figure 5.4 Anchor Chart

Exploring Arrays

Build with concrete materials

Sketch

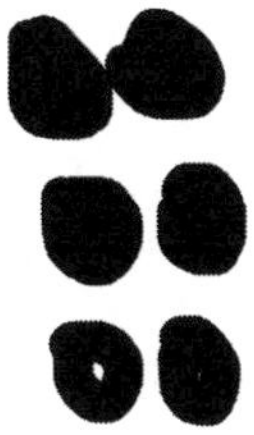

Write the Numbers to Represent the Array

- 3 groups of 2
- $3 \times 2 = 6$

Concrete Lesson

Figure 5.5 Concrete Introduction

	Introduction to Arrays
Launch	**Teacher:** Today we are going to work on building arrays. **Vocabulary:** array, expression, equation, product, factors, columns, rows, equal groups **Math Talk:** The array is ____ by ____. The factors are ___ and ___. The product is _____.
Model	Teacher: Today we are going to building arrays in different ways. The array is 6. Build it in 2 ways.

Way 1	Way 2
● ● ● ● ● ●	● ● ● ● ● ●
$3 + 3$ 2 groups of 3 2×3	$2 + 2 + 2$ 3 groups of 2 3×2

Checking for Understanding	**Teacher:** Ok, so I am going to give each one of you a problem to solve. I want you to solve it any way you want and then explain it back to the group. Model it with your virtual manipulatives.

Figure 5.6 Student Activity

	Concrete Student Activity
Guided Practice/ Checking for Understanding	As the students work, the teacher watches, takes notes and asks them questions. **Teacher**: Todd explain what you did. **Todd:** I had 2 × 4. **Teacher:** How did you build your array? **Todd:** I made 2 groups of 4 for way 1. Then, I made 4 groups of 2.

Way 1	Way 2
●●●● ●●●●	●● ●● ●● ●●
4 + 4 2 groups of 4 2 × 4	2 + 2 + 2 + 2 4 groups of 2 4 × 2

Set up for Independent Practice	Every child shares out their problem and how they solved it. We are going to be talking more about this in the upcoming days. Are there any questions? What was interesting today? What was tricky?

Figure 5.7 Lesson Close

Close
• What did we do today?
• What was the math we were practicing?
• How did we model the math?
• Was this easy or tricky?
• Turn to a partner and state one thing you learned today.

Figure 5.8 Array Cards

2 x 2	2 x 3	2 x 4
2 x 5	2 x 6	2 x 7
2 x 8	2 x 9	2 x 10
2 x 2	2 x 3	2 x 4
3 x 5	3 x 6	3 x 7
3 x 8	3 x 9	3 x 10

Visual Lesson

Figure 5.9 Visual Introduction

<table>
<tr>
<td colspan="2" align="center"><h2>Introduction to Visual Explorations</h2></td>
</tr>
<tr>
<td>Launch</td>
<td>

Teacher: Today we are going to work on building arrays.

Vocabulary: array, expression, equation, product, factors, groups of, multiply, equal groups, total

Math Talk:
I see _____ groups of _____.

</td>
</tr>
<tr>
<td>Model</td>
<td>

Teacher: What do you see? How do you see it?

Yesenia: On Card 1 see 3 groups of 2. I see 3 × 2. I see a total of 6 dots.

Marcos: On card 2, I see 2 groups of 3. I see 2 × 3. I see 6 dots

Card 1	Card 2

</td>
</tr>
<tr>
<td>Checking for Understanding</td>
<td>

Teacher: I am going to give each one of you a problem. I want you to tell us what you see and explain your thinking.

</td>
</tr>
</table>

Figure 5.10 Student Activity

	Visual Student Activity
Guided Practice/ Checking for Understanding	**Teacher:** Who wants to go first? **Dan:** I do. On card 1, I see 3 groups of 3. I see 3×3. There are 9. **Marta:** On Card 2, I see 2 groups of 4. I see 8. 2×4 is 8. <table><tr><td>Card 1</td><td>Card 2</td></tr></table>
Set up for Independent Practice	*Teacher gives everybody a chance to do and discuss a problem. After everyone has shared the lesson ends.* We are going to be talking more about that in the upcoming days. Are there any questions? What was interesting today? What was tricky?

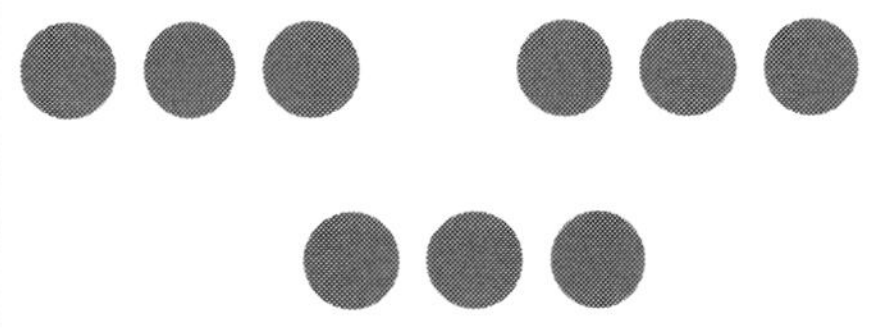

Figure 5.11 Lesson Close

Close
• What did we do today? • What was the math we were practicing? • How did we model the math? • Was this easy or tricky? • Turn to a partner and state one thing you learned today.

Figure 5.12 Multiplication Subitizing Cards

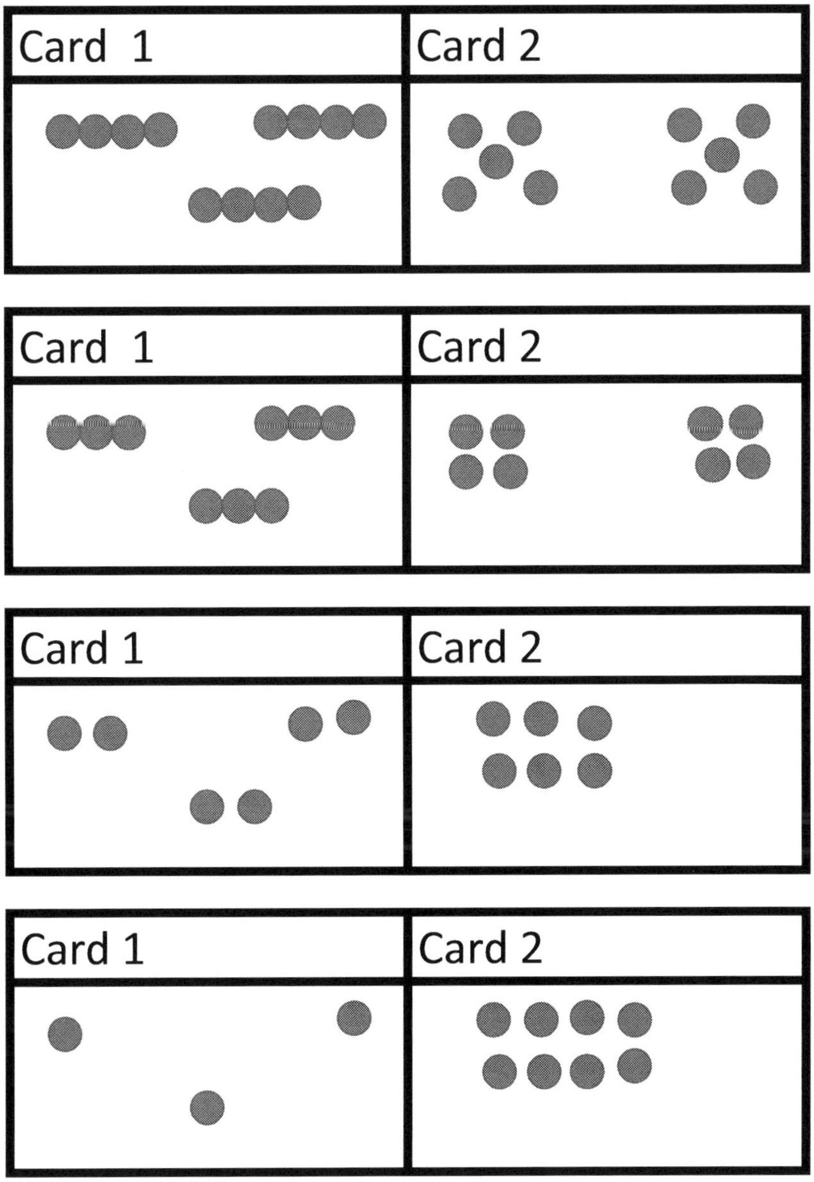

Abstract Lesson

Figure 5.13 Abstract Introduction

	Introduction to Abstract Explorations
Launch	**Teacher:** Today we are going to work on talking about multiplication problems. **Vocabulary:** array, expression, equation, product, factors **Math Talk:** The factors are ___ and ___. The product is _____. This is tricky because _____.
Model	**Teacher:** Look at this card and think about which problem is tricky for you and why? **What's tricky?** 8 x 8 4 x 4 3 x 5 **Why? What's your strategy?** **Joe:** I think 8 × 8 is tricky. It's big. **Tina:** Yea, I don't know my 8's. **Marta:** That's tricky for me too! **Teacher:** I have a question for you all. What is a strategy that could help you? Remember we talked about strategy (a way to think about it) to try and figure out the fact. **Tom:** I know. We could think about what is 4 × 8. And then double it! **Teacher:** Bingo. Remember, if you can't remember your 8's (and lots of people think those are tricky) you can always use your strategies. Tell me how that might sound. **Tina:** 4 × 8 is 32. So 8 times 8 is 64. **Teacher:** Yes! Let's do another one.
Checking for Understanding	**Teacher:** Yes! Let's do another one. I am going to give each one of you a card with different multiplication facts. I want you to think about which of the facts are tricky and share the strategy you could use to help you solve that fact.

Figure 5.14 Abstract Student Activity

	Abstract Student Activity
Guided Practice/ Checking for Understanding	**Teacher:** What's tricky? **What's tricky?** | 8 x 5	4 x 5	6 x 5 | Why? What's your strategy? **Kayla:** 8×5 **John:** 8×5 **Luke:** 8×5 **Terri:** But if 4×5 is 20 then 8×5 is 40. **Teacher:** Great use of a strategy. You used the relationship of doubles.
Set up for Independent Practice	The students come up with the answers and explain what they did. Teacher explains that this activity will be one of the choices in the workstations and that they should talk through different strategies with their math buddies.

Figure 5.15 Lesson Close

Close
• What did we do today? • What was the math we were practicing? • How did we model the math? • Was this easy or tricky? • Turn to a partner and state one thing you learned today.

Figure 5.16 What's Tricky? (download all the cards)

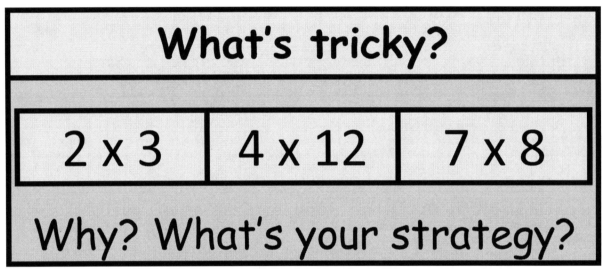

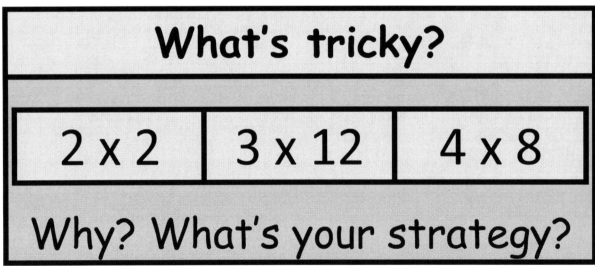

Section Summary

Students need to understand how to build and draw arrays. They need to know how to subitize groups and write the verbal statement and the multiplication equation. They must be able to reason about strategies. These are a few lessons that show what that might look like in the guided math group. The emphasis here is on a cycle of concrete, pictorial and abstract activities so that students can visualize the math and use that to build a strong conceptual foundation for multiplication.

Overview

Figure 5.17 Introduction Circle

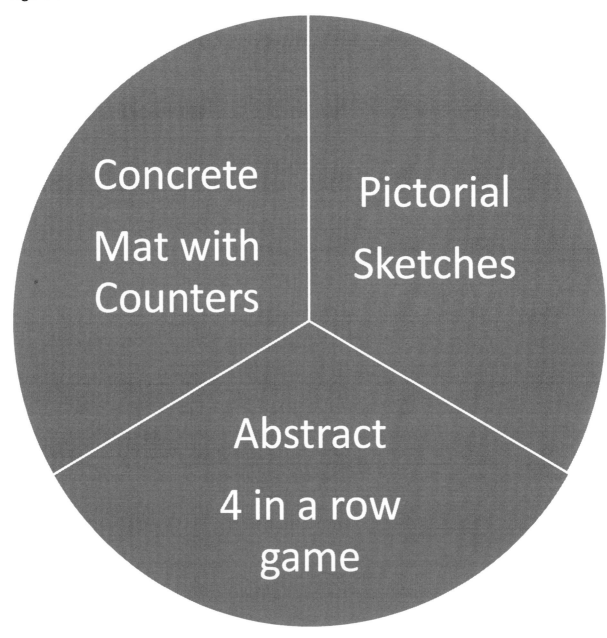

Figure 5.18 Planning Template

Division Mats	
Big Idea: Numbers, Operation Meanings & Relationships; Properties, Basic Facts & Algorithms **Enduring Understanding**: Students will understand that dividing can be sharing equally. **Essential Question**: Why is division important? How do we use it in real life? **I can statement**: I can model division problems. I can divide and explain my work.	**Materials** • Tools: counters (tiles, cubes, circles)
Cycle of Engagement Concrete: Pictorial: Abstract: $9 \div 3 =$	**Vocabulary & Language Frames** **Vocabulary:** factors, array, product, row, column, horizontal, vertical **Math Talk:** They array is ___ by ____. There are ___ columns and ____ rows. **Math Processes/Practices** • Problem Solving • Reasoning • Models • Tools • Precision • Structure • Pattern

Figure 5.19 Differentiated Lessons

Three Differentiated Lessons		
In this series of lessons, students are working on dividing. They are developing this concept through concrete activities, pictorial activities and abstract activities. Here are some things to think about as you do these lessons.		
Emerging	**On Grade Level**	**Above Grade Level**
Division is more challenging than multiplication. Review subtraction. Also, do a great deal of problems using small numbers so students can visualize the math.	Students should work on understanding concepts such as what happens when 0 is divided by a number, what happens when dividing by 1, 2, the number itself etc. They should also understand and be able to explain the properties of division.	When students know their division facts within 100, then they should begin exploring by 11 and 12.
WATCH OUT Looking for Misunderstandings and Common Errors		
Students have trouble with division. It is important to use division math mats with them because it helps them to physically act out the story as it is being told. After they do that, then they can do sketches. After they do that, they can move on to tape/bar/strip diagrams.		

Figure 5.20 Anchor Chart

Modeling Division

Concrete:

Pictorial:

Abstract:

$$6 \div 2 = 3$$

Concrete Lesson

Figure 5.21 Concrete Introduction

Introduction to Concrete Explorations
I am learning to add a 10 more to a number

Launch	**Teacher:** Today we are going to work on division. **Vocabulary:** dividend, divisor, quotient, expression, equation, share equally **Math Talk:** The quotient is _____. The dividend is ____. The divisor is ____.
Model	**Teacher:** We are going to be telling division stories. We will act them out on our mats. <table><tr><td colspan="4">There are 4 kids. There are 4 donuts. How many donuts does each kid get?</td></tr><tr><td></td><td></td><td></td><td></td></tr><tr><td>●</td><td>●</td><td>●</td><td>●</td></tr><tr><td colspan="4">Equation: 4 ÷ 4 = 1</td></tr></table>
Checking for Understanding	**Teacher:** Ok. I am going to give each one of you your own problem. I want you to read it. Solve it. Be ready to share how you did it. I am going to watch you and if you need help, look at our anchor charts and of course you can ask me.

Figure 5.22 Student Activity

	Concrete Student Activity
Guided Practice/ Checking for Understanding	The teacher reads one more problem that the students do together then they each get their own cards to work on. As they do their work, the teacher takes notes, asks questions and has a conversation with individual students. **Teacher:** Tell us about your problem. **Kayla:** There were 4 kids, so each kid gets 2 donuts. I shared them equally. The equation is 8 divided by 4  There are 4 kids. There are 8 donuts. How many donuts does each kid get if they shared them equally? Equation: 8 ÷ 4 = 2
Set up for Independent Practice	Every child shares out their problem and how they solved it their problem. **Teacher:** We are going to be talking more about this in the upcoming days. Are there any questions? What was interesting today? What was tricky?

Visual Lesson

Figure 5.23 Lesson Close

Close
• What did we do today? • What was the math we were practicing? • How did we model the math? • Was this easy or tricky? • Turn to a partner and state one thing you learned today.

Figure 5.24 Division Mat Cards

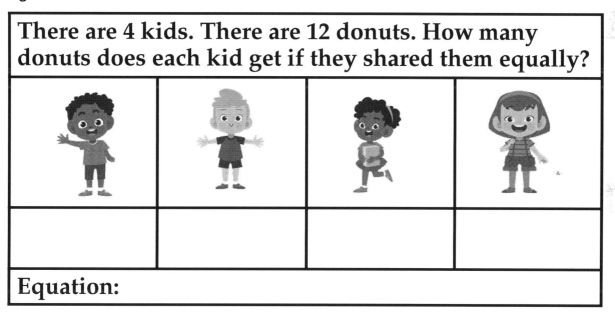

There are 4 kids. There are 12 donuts. How many donuts does each kid get if they shared them equally?			
Equation:			

Figure 5.25 Visual Introduction

Introduction to a Visual Explorations	
Launch	**Teacher:** Today we are going to work on division. **Vocabulary:** dividend, divisor, quotient, expression, equation, shared equally **Math Talk:** The quotient is _____. The dividend is ____. The divisor is ____.
Model	**Teacher:** Today we are going to be working on division strips to show division problems. Let's look at this one. We are going to divide by 5 today. There were 5 children. There were 15 oranges. How many oranges did each child get if they shared them equally? **Luke:** I drew 5 kids and then I shared out the oranges. Each kid got 3.
Checking for Understanding	**Teacher:** Ok. I am going to give each one of you your own problem. I want you to read it. Solve it. Be ready to share how you did it. I am going to watch you and if you need help, look at our anchor charts and of course you can ask me.

Figure 5.26 Student Activity

Visual Student Activities	
Guided Practice/ Checking for Understanding	**Lara:** My problem said there were 5 children. They had 10 oranges. How many did each child get if they shared them equality? I drew 5 kids and then I shared out the oranges. Each kid got 2. 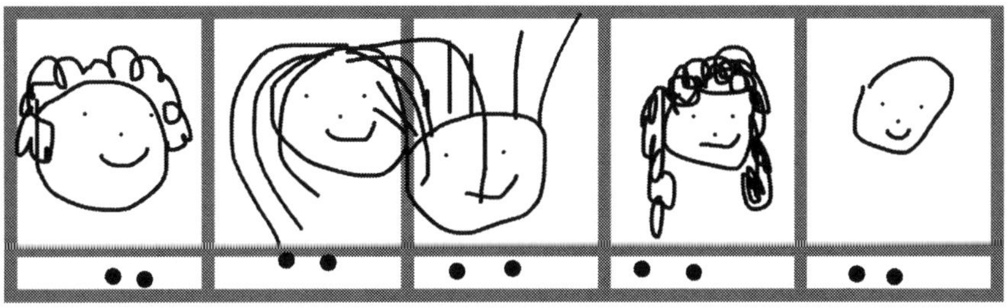
Set up for Independent Practice	Every child shares out their problem and how they solved it. **Teacher:** We are going to be talking more about that in the upcoming days. Are there any questions? What was interesting today? What was tricky?

Figure 5.27 Lesson Close

Close
• What did we do today?   • What was the math we were practicing?   • How did we model the math?   • Was this easy or tricky?   • Turn to a partner and state one thing you used today.

Abstract Lesson

Figure 5.28 Abstract Introduction

	Introduction to Abstract Explorations
Launch	**Teacher:** Today we are going to continue to work on division. **Vocabulary:** dividend, divisor, quotient, expression, equation **Math Talk:** The quotient is _____. The dividend is _____. The divisor is _____.
Model	**Teacher:** We are going to play a 4 in a row game. So you pull a card and divide that number by 5. Cover the quotient. Whoever gets 4 in a row wins. So if I pulled 40, what could I cover? **Diamond:** You could cover 8 because 40 divided by 5 is 8. <table><tr><td>1</td><td>2</td><td>3</td><td>5</td><td>4</td></tr><tr><td>10</td><td>6</td><td>7</td><td>8</td><td>9</td></tr><tr><td>8</td><td>5</td><td>11</td><td>9</td><td>12</td></tr><tr><td>3</td><td>10</td><td>2</td><td>11</td><td>7</td></tr><tr><td>5</td><td>6</td><td>9</td><td>12</td><td>8</td></tr><tr><td>10</td><td>2</td><td>7</td><td>1</td><td>6</td></tr></table>
Checking for Understanding	**Teacher:** What if I pulled 20 and I was stuck? What strategy could help me? **Kim:** You could think multiplication. 5 × what number makes 20. That's 4. **Teacher:** Yes! So we can use multiplication to help us with our division problems. We have been practicing that during energizers.

Figure 5.29 Student Activity

Abstract Student Activity	
Guided Practice/ Checking for Understanding	The teacher watches partners play the game, takes notes, writes comments and asks questions. **Teacher:** Todd and Taylor tell me what just happened in your game. **Todd:** I pulled 35 so I covered 7.

1	2	3	5	4
10	6	7	8	9
8	5	11	9	12
3	10	2	11	7
5	6	9	12	8
10	2	7	1	6

Taylor: I pulled 15 so I covered 3.
Teacher: Why did you cover 3?
Taylor: Because 15 divided by 5 is 3. |
| **Set up for Independent Practice** | After all the students share, the teacher wraps up the lesson and the students go to their workstations. |

Figure 5.30 Lesson Close

Close
• What did we do today? • What was the math we were practicing? • How did we model the math? • Was this easy or tricky? • Turn to a partner and state one thing you learned today.

Figure 5.31 4 in a Row Game

Divide by 5 Four in a Row

Directions: Play rock, paper, scissors to see who starts first. Take turns. Pull a card and divide that number by 5. Find the quotient. Cover that space with a counter. Each player should have their own specific color of counter. Whoever gets 4 in a row first wins.

1	2	3	5	4
10	6	7	8	9
8	5	11	9	12
3	10	2	11	7
5	6	9	12	8
10	2	7	1	6

5	10	15	20	25
30	35	40	45	50

Section Summary

Division is tricky for students. They must have plenty of opportunities where they get to act out word problems. The problems should be real-life contexts so that students can understand what they are talking about. They should act out the problem with manipulatives, then sketch out the problems and finally be able to solve the problems with symbols. Students should be able to talk about the relationships between concrete, pictorial and abstract representations of the same problem.

Overview

Figure 5.32 Overview

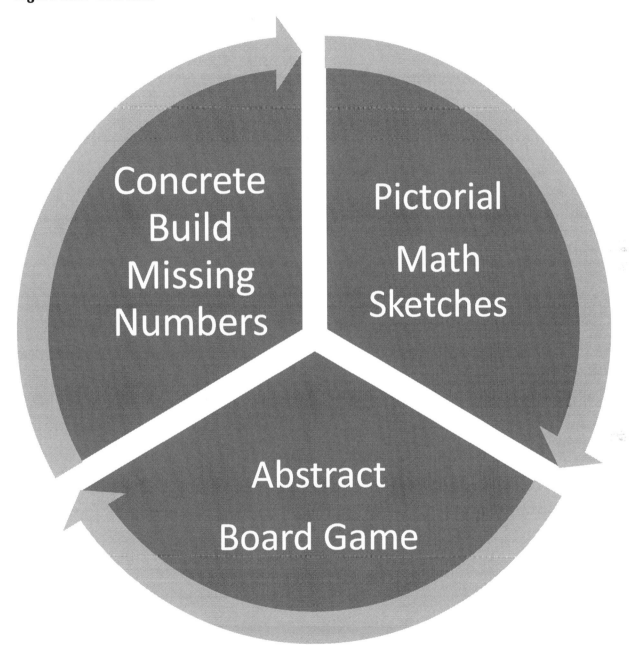

Figure 5.33 Planning Template

Missing Numbers

Big Idea: Numbers, Operation Meanings & Relationships; Properties, Basic Facts & Algorithms

Enduring Understanding: Students will understand that they can solve for missing numbers in an equation using relationships between operations.

Essential Question: What is multiplication? Which operation is related to multiplication? How can addition help us when we are multiplying? What are different ways to think about solving for missing numbers?

I can statement: I can find missing numbers in equations.

Materials
- Tools: counters (tiles, cubes, circles)

Vocabulary & Language Frames

Vocabulary: factors, array, product, row, column, horizontal, vertical

Math Talk:
They array is ___ by ____.
There are ___ columns and ____ rows.

Cycle of Engagement
Concrete: $2 \times ? = 6$

Pictorial: $2 \times ? = 6$

Abstract:
$2 \times ? = 6$
2 groups of what equals 6
$2 \times 3 = 6$

Math Processes/Practices
- **Problem Solving**
- **Reasoning**
- **Models**
- **Tools**
- **Precision**
- **Structure**
- **Pattern**

Figure 5.34 Differentiated Lessons

Three Differentiated Lessons
In this series of lessons, students are working on finding missing numbers in equations. They are developing this concept through concrete activities, pictorial activities and abstract activities. Here are some things to think about as you do these lessons.

Emerging	On Grade Level	Above Grade Level
Do a lot of work with manipulatives. Students should have to reason about the equations. Make sure that students can reason about addition and subtraction equations well. This was introduced in first grade but many students still struggle with meaning of equality.	Do a lot of work with different manipulatives and having the students do math sketches. They should have to defend their thinking with manipulatives and sketches. They must explain their thinking.	Continue to work on this with larger numbers as they master the concept. So for example: $11 \times 3 = (12 \times 2) + \_\_$. Have students reason out the answer.

 Looking for Misunderstandings and Common Errors

Students find missing number problems tricky. Do a lot of problems where they have to use manipulatives and number lines to count up and count back.

Figure 5.35 Anchor Chart

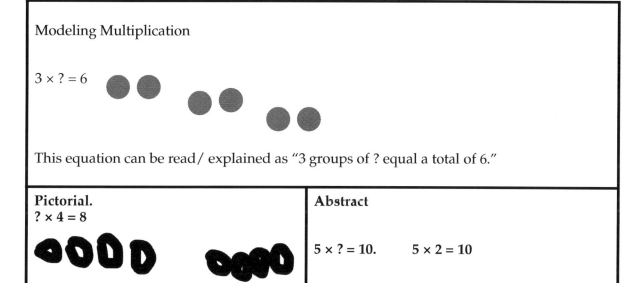

Modeling Multiplication

$3 \times ? = 6$

This equation can be read/ explained as "3 groups of ? equal a total of 6."

Pictorial.
$? \times 4 = 8$

This equation can be read/ explained as "How many groups of 4 would equal 8?"

Abstract

$5 \times ? = 10.$ $5 \times 2 = 10$

This equation can be read/ explained as "5 groups of ? equal a total of 10"

Figure 5.36 Concrete Introduction

Introduction to Concrete Explorations
I am learning to find missing numbers in multiplication equations.

Launch	**Teacher:** Today we are going to work on finding missing numbers
	Vocabulary: product, factors, groups of, multiplication, multiply expression, equation, missing number
	Math Talk:
	• The factors are _____.
	• The product is _____.
	• The missing factor is _____.
Model	**Teacher:** We are going to work on finding missing numbers.
	Use your counters to figure out the problem!
	3 groups of ? = 6
	$3 \times ? = 6$
	Juan: 3 groups of 2. **Maite:** Are you sure? **Juan:** Yes see ... 3 groups and 2 in each group makes 6.
Checking for Understanding	*Teacher reads 2 more problems that the group discusses.*
	Teacher: Ok. I am going to give each one of you your own problem. I want you to read it. Solve it. Be ready to share how you did it. I am going to watch you and if you need help, look at our anchor charts and of course you can ask me.

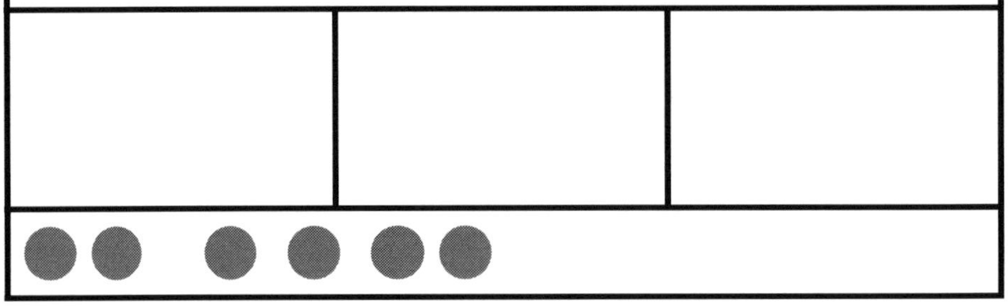

Concrete Lesson

Figure 5.37 Student Activity

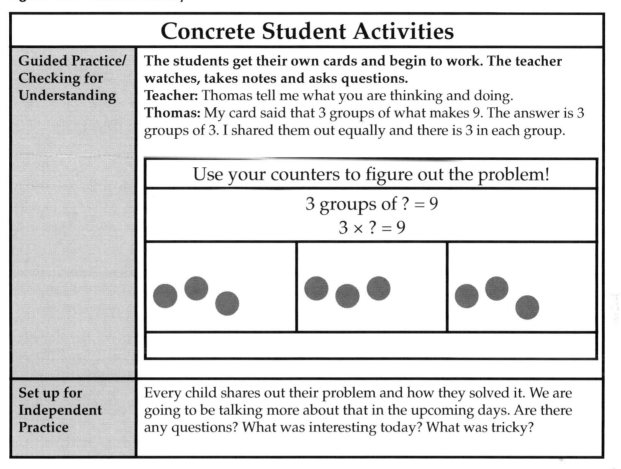

	Concrete Student Activities
Guided Practice/ Checking for Understanding	The students get their own cards and begin to work. The teacher watches, takes notes and asks questions. **Teacher:** Thomas tell me what you are thinking and doing. **Thomas:** My card said that 3 groups of what makes 9. The answer is 3 groups of 3. I shared them out equally and there is 3 in each group.
Set up for Independent Practice	Every child shares out their problem and how they solved it. We are going to be talking more about that in the upcoming days. Are there any questions? What was interesting today? What was tricky?

Within the middle section:

Use your counters to figure out the problem!

3 groups of ? = 9

$3 \times ? = 9$

Figure 5.38 Lesson Close

Close

- What did we do today?
- What was the math we were practicing?
- What were we doing with our number wands?
- Was this easy or tricky?
- Turn to a partner and state one thing you learned today.

Visual Lesson

Figure 5.39 Missing Addend Cards (download these)

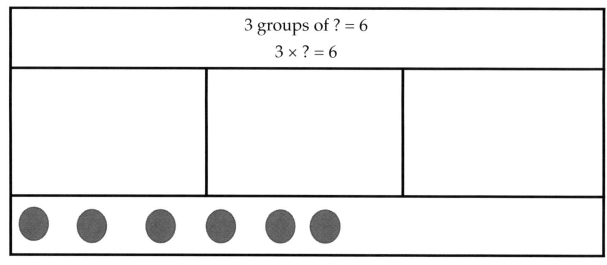

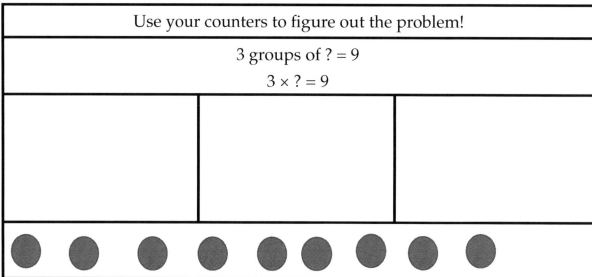

Figure 5.40 Visual Introduction

	## Introduction to a Visual Explorations
Launch	**Teacher:** Today we are going to work on finding missing numbers. **Vocabulary:** product, factors, groups of, multiplication, multiply expression, equation, missing number **Math Talk:** • The factors are _____. • The product is _____. • The missing factor is _____.
Model	**Teacher:** We are going to work on finding missing factors in multiplication equations by using math sketches. Everybody try and then somebody share your thinking. **Mary:** I'll share. I just counted them out giving 1 to each one until I counted 12. I got 3 in each group. **Joey:** Me too! Make a math sketch to figure out the problem! 4 groups of ? = 12 $4 \times ? = 12$ 4 × 3 = 12
Checking for Understanding	**Teacher:** Ok. I am going to give each one of you your own problem. I want you to read it. Solve it. Be ready to share how you did it. I am going to watch you and if you need help, look at our anchor charts and of course you can ask me.

Figure 5.41 Student Activity

	Visual Student Activity
Guided Practice/ Checking for Understanding	The students get their own cards and begin to work. The teacher watches, takes notes and asks questions. **Teacher:** Nikeli tell me what you are thinking and doing. **Nikeli:** I know that 4×2 is 8. 4 groups of 2 make 8. So I used my multiplication facts but I also modeled it with a sketch. **Make a math sketch to figure out the problem!** 4 groups of ? = 8 $4 \times ? = 8$  4 × 2 = 8
Set up for Independent Practice	*Teacher gives everybody a chance to do and discuss a problem. After everyone has shared the lesson ends.* *Teacher: We are going to be talking more about that in the upcoming days. Are there any questions? What was interesting today? What was tricky?*

Figure 5.42 Lesson Close

Close
• What did we do today? • What was the math we were practicing? • What were we doing with our number wands? • Was this easy or tricky? • Turn to a partner and state one thing you learned today.

Figure 5.43 Missing Number Cards

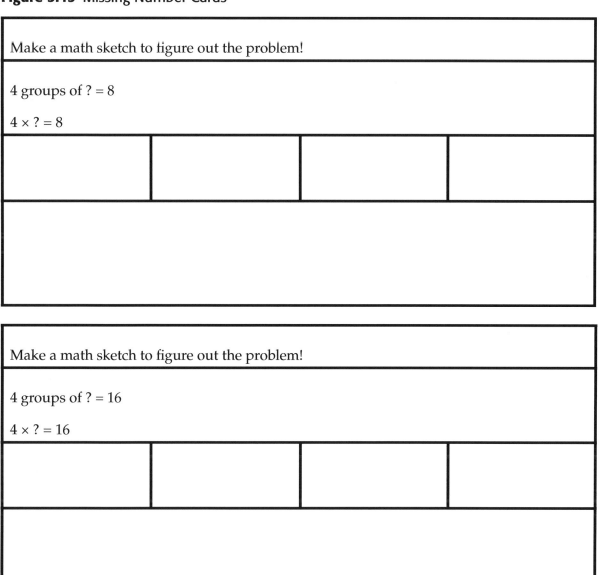

Abstract Lesson

Figure 5.44 Abstract Introduction

Introduction to Abstract Explorations

Launch	**Teacher:** Today we are going to work on multiplication.. **Vocabulary:** product, factors, groups of, multiplication, multiply expression, equation **Math Talk:** • The factors are _____. • The product is ____. • The missing factor is ____.
Model	**Teacher:** We are going to play a multiplication board game where you are looking for the missing number. You roll the dice and move around the board. You answer the questions. There is a missing number. If you get it correct you stay there. If you miss it, you move back one space. 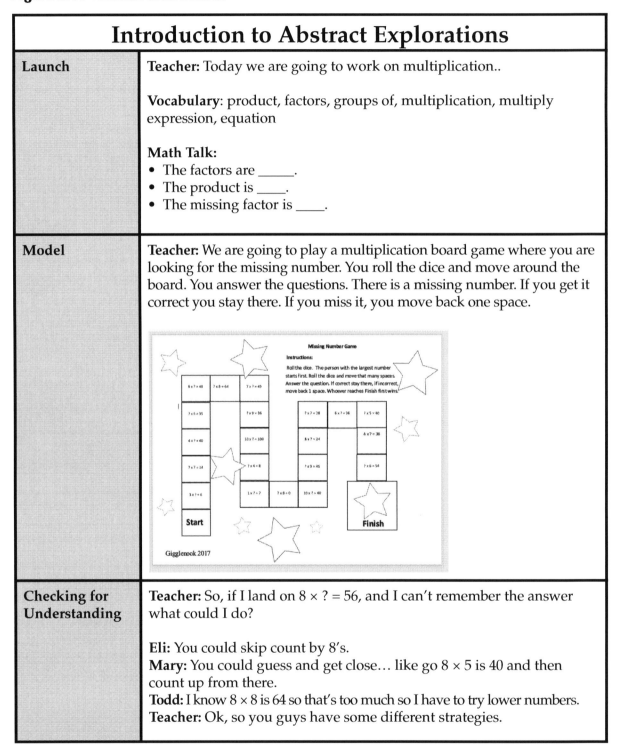
Checking for Understanding	**Teacher:** So, if I land on 8 × ? = 56, and I can't remember the answer what could I do? **Eli:** You could skip count by 8's. **Mary:** You could guess and get close... like go 8 × 5 is 40 and then count up from there. **Todd:** I know 8 × 8 is 64 so that's too much so I have to try lower numbers. **Teacher:** Ok, so you guys have some different strategies.

Figure 5.44a

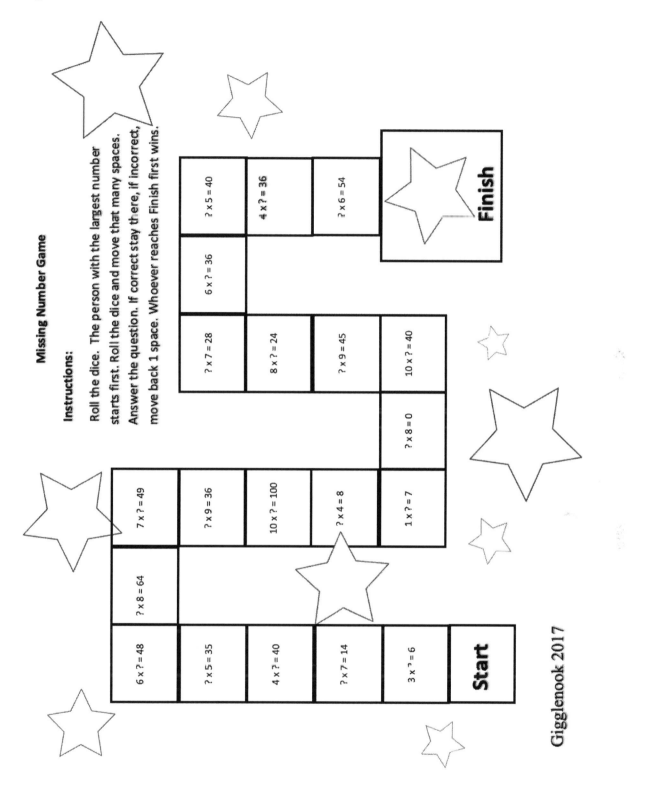

Missing Number Game

Instructions:

Roll the dice. The person with the largest number starts first. Roll the dice and move that many spaces. Answer the question. If correct stay there, if incorrect, move back 1 space. Whoever reaches Finish first wins.

Finish

? x 5 = 40
4 x ? = 36
? x 6 = 54

6 x ? = 36

? x 7 = 28
8 x ? = 24
? x 9 = 45
10 x ? = 40

? x 8 = 0

7 x ? = 49
? x 9 = 36
10 x ? = 100
? x 4 = 8
1 x ? = 7

? x 8 = 64

6 x ? = 48
? x 5 = 35
4 x ? = 40
? x 7 = 14
3 x ? = 6
Start

Gigglenook 2017

Figure 5.45 Abstract Student Activity

Abstract Student Activity	
Guided Practice/ Checking for Understanding	Teacher watches the students play the game and asks them some questions. **Teacher:** Tiffany, tell me how you solved that problem. **Tiffany:** My problem is $2 \times ? = 10$. I just know it, that 2×5 is 10. But if I didn't know it, I could skip count by 2's to figure it out.
Set up for Independent Practice	The teacher continues to ask the students questions about their strategies as they play the game. The teacher is taking notes as the students play. They are using their different strategies to explain their thinking.

Figure 5.46 Lesson Close

Close
• What did we do today? • What was the math we were practicing? • How did we model the math? • Was this easy or tricky? • Turn to a partner and state one thing you learned today.

Section Summary

Finding the missing number is tricky for many students. Students tend to want to work with both of the numbers on either side of the equal sign to come up with just any answer. It is important that they have templates and diagrams to act out the situations so they can see the math in action. When they do this, they should be talking through their thinking and then later be able to sketch it, without using the manipulatives. They should be able to talk about what the numbers in the equation mean and also the strategies that they would use to figure out the missing numbers.

Splitting Arrays

Overview

Figure 5.47 Overview

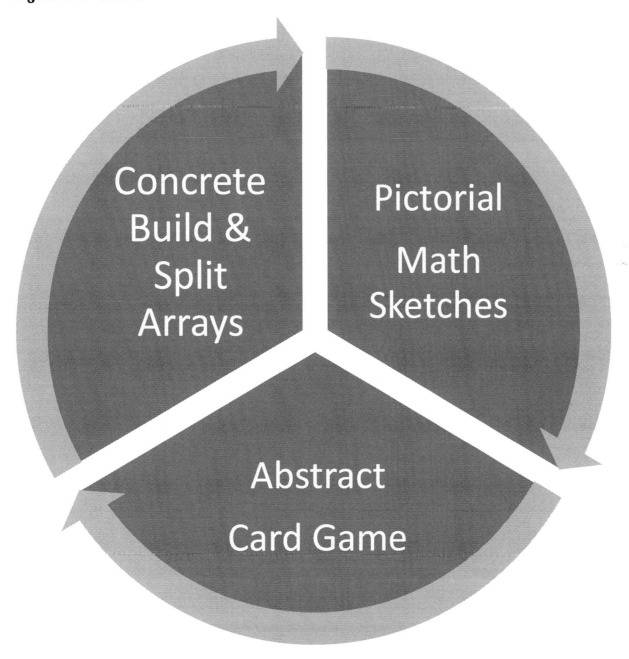

Figure 5.48 Planning Template

Build and Split Arrays

Big Idea: Numbers, Operation Meanings & Relationships; Properties, Basic Facts & Algorithms

Enduring Understanding: Students will understand that arrays can be split apart into different equations using the distributive property.

Essential Question: What is multiplication? How can addition help us when we are multiplying? What are different ways to think about splitting arrays?

I can statement: I can show the distributive property with different models.

Materials
- Tools: counters (tiles, cubes, circles)

Vocabulary & Language Frames

Vocabulary: factors, array, product, row, column, horizontal, vertical, equal groups

Math Talk:
They array is ___ by ____.
There are ___ columns and ____ rows.
My original expression was _____.
I split my array and now it is _____.

Cycle of Engagement

$$2 \times 4 = (2 \times 2) + (2 \times 2)$$

Concrete: 2×4

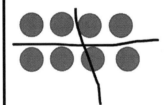

Pictorial:

Abstract:
$2 \times 4 = (2 \times 2) + (2 \times 2) = 8$

Math Processes/Practices
- **Problem Solving**
- **Reasoning**
- **Models**
- **Tools**
- **Precision**
- **Structure**
- **Pattern**

Figure 5.49 Differentiated Lessons

Three Differentiated Lessons
In this series of lessons, students are working on breaking apart arrays (working on the distributive property). They are developing this concept through concrete activities, pictorial activities and abstract activities. Here are some things to think about as you do these lessons.

Emerging	On Grade Level	Above Grade Level
Do a lot of work with manipulatives. Scaffold understanding by using 1 inch tiles, and then 1 inch grid paper to model breaking apart arrays. In the beginning work with smaller numbers.	Have students work with different manipulatives, (cubes, tiles, bears) putting them in arrays and breaking them apart. Be sure that they are working with 1 inch grid and centimeter paper to visually illustrate the process. Make sure that students can make up and solve their own problems.	Continue to work with this idea with larger numbers, including 11's and 12's.

 Looking for Misunderstandings and Common Errors

Students find the distributive property to be tricky. Do a lot of problems where they have to use manipulatives and then sketch and explain their work. Start with small numbers so they can visualize what they are doing.

Figure 5.50 Anchor Chart

Modeling Multiplication

$3 \times 4 = 12$

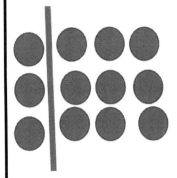

$3 \times 4 = (3 \times 1) + (3 \times 3)$

Pictorial.	**Abstract**
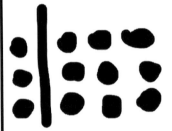	$3 \times 4 = (3 \times 1) + (3 \times 3)$

Concrete Lesson

Figure 5.51 Concrete Introduction

	Introduction to a Concrete Exploration
Launch	**Teacher:** Today we are going to work on the distributive property. **Vocabulary**: product, factors, groups of, multiplication, multiply expression, equation **Math Talk:** • The factors are _____. • The product is ____. • The original equation was____. • I split up the numbers into
Model	**Teacher:** Today we are going to look at what happens when we break apart an array. Look at this example. Who can explain it? **Terri:** You broke up 2 groups of 3 into 2 groups of 1 plus 2 groups of 2. <table><tr><td>**Array 1**</td><td>**Break it up!**</td></tr><tr><td>■ ■ ■ ■ ■ ■</td><td>■ ■ ■ ■ ■ ■</td></tr><tr><td>**2 × 3**</td><td>**(2 × 1) + (2 × 2)**</td></tr></table>
Checking for Understanding	**Teacher:** Ok. I am going to give each one of you your own problem. I want you to read it. Solve it. Be ready to share how you did it. I am going to watch you and if you need help, look at our anchor charts and of course you can ask me.

Figure 5.52 Student Activity

	Concrete Student Activity
Guided Practice/ Checking for Understanding	The students get their own cards and begin to work. The teacher watches, takes notes and asks questions. **Teacher:** Harry tell me what you are thinking and doing. **Harry:** I had 2 groups of 4 and I broke it up into 2 groups of 2 plus 2 groups of 2.

Array 1	Break it up!
2×4	$(2 \times 2) + (2 \times 2)$

Set up for Independent Practice	*Teacher gives everybody a chance to do and discuss a problem. After everyone has shared the lesson ends.* *Teacher: We are going to be talking more about that in the upcoming days. Are there any questions? What was interesting today? What was tricky?*

Figure 5.53 Lesson Close

Close
• What did we do today? • What was the math we were practicing? • How did we model the math? • Was this easy or tricky? • Turn to a partner and state one thing you learned today.

Figure 5.54 Array Break Up Card

Array 1	Break it up!
_____ × _____	(_____×_____) + (_____×_____)

Visual Lesson

Figure 5.55 Visual Introduction

Introduction to a Visual Explorations

Launch	**Teacher:** Today we are going to work on the distributive property.. **Vocabulary**: product, factors, groups of, multiplication, multiply expression, equation **Math Talk:** • The factors are _____. • The product is ____. • The original equation was____. • I split ____ and _____.
Model	**Teacher:** Look at my template. My original problem was 2 × 4. I drew it and then split it and now I have (2 × 2) + (2 × 2). <table><tr><td>**Draw an array and split it!**</td></tr><tr><td> </td></tr><tr><td>$(2 \times 2) + (2 \times 2) = 8$</td></tr><tr><td></td></tr></table>

Checking for Understanding	**Teacher:** Who wants to go next?
	Kayla: I do. I had 2 × 6 and I split it into (1 × 6) and (1 × 6).

Draw an array and split it!

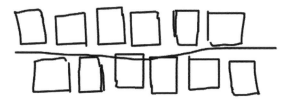

$$(1 \times 6) + (1 \times 6) = 12$$

Teacher: Excellent. Does anybody see another way we could split it?

Dan: Yes. I split it into (2 × 3) plus (2 × 3).

Draw an array and split it!

$$(2 \times 3) + (2 \times 3)$$

Figure 5.56 Student Activity

<center>**Pictorial Student Activity**</center>	
Guided Practice/ Checking for Understanding	Teacher watches the students work on problem and takes notes and engages in conversation about the work. **Teacher:** Dante tell me about your picture. Dante: I had 2 times 5. I broke it apart into 1 × 5 plus 1 × 5. I got 10. <table><tr><td>**Draw an array and split it!**</td></tr><tr><td>$$2 \times 5 = (1 \times 5) + (1 \times 5)$$</td></tr></table>
Set up for Independent Practice	*Teacher gives everybody a chance to do and discuss a problem. After everyone has shared the lesson ends.* We are going to be talking more about that in the upcoming days. Are there any questions? What was interesting today? What was tricky?

Figure 5.57 Lesson Close

Close
• What did we do today? • What was the math we were practicing? • How did we model the math? • Was this easy or tricky? • Turn to a partner and state one thing you learned today.

Figure 5.58 Split Array Template

Draw an array and split it!
Drawing:
Equation

Abstract Lesson

Figure 5.59 Abstract Introduction

	Introduction to Abstract Explorations
Launch	**Teacher:** Today we are going to work on the distributive property. **Vocabulary:** product, factors, groups of, multiplication, multiply expression, equation **Math Talk:** The factors are _____. The product is ____. The original equation was____. I split my equation into ____ and ____.
Model	**Teacher:** Today we are going to play a concentration game. You are looking for equivalent expressions. For example, these would be a match because they equal the same amount. 2×4 $(2 \times 2) + (2 \times 2)$
Checking for Understanding	**Teacher:** Who can find another pair that would go together? (students look through their cards that are in a baggie) **Maite:** I found a match. 3×4 $(3 \times 2) + (3 \times 2)$

Figure 5.60 Student Activity

Abstract Student Activity	
Guided Practice/ Checking for Understanding	**Teacher watches pairs of students work together and asks them about their work.** **Teacher:** Don and Miguel explain your thinking. **Don:** We found this is a matching pair. 24 is the same as 12 + 12. 6×4 $(6 \times 2) + (6 \times 2)$ **Tiffany:** This is not a match. 12×4 does not equal $4 + 4$. 48 does not equal 8 12×4 $(2 \times 2) + (2 \times 2)$
Set up for Independent Practice	The teacher continues to ask the students questions about their strategies as they play the game. The teacher is taking notes as the students play. They are using their different strategies to explain their thinking.

Figure 5.61 Lesson Close

Close
• What did we do today? • What was the math we were practicing? • How did we model the math? • Was this easy or tricky? • Turn to a partner and state one thing you learned today.

Figure 5.62 Concentration/Match Cards (download these)

2 × 6	(2 × 3)+ (2 × 3)
4 × 8	(4 × 4)+ (4 × 4)
3 × 9	(3 × 4)+ (3 × 5)
12 × 4	(12 × 2)+ (12 × 2)
5 × 10	(5 × 5)+ (5 × 5)

Section Summary

Working with the distributive property is tricky for many students. It is important that they have templates and diagrams to act out the situations so they can see the math in action. When they do this, they should be talking through their thinking and then later be able to sketch it, without using the manipulatives. They should be able to talk about what the numbers in the equation mean and also the strategies that they would use to figure out different ways to split the array.

Depth of Knowledge

Depth of Knowledge is a framework that encourages us to ask questions that require that students think, reason, explain, defend and justify their thinking (Webb, 2002). Here is snapshot of what that can look like in terms of multiplication work.

Figure 5.63 DOK Activities

	What are different strategies and models that we can use to teach arrays?	What are different strategies and models that we can use to teach division?	What are different strategies and models to teach missing numbers?	What are different strategies and models to teach the distributive property?
DOK Level 1 (These are questions where students are required to simply recall/reproduce an answer/do a procedure.)	Draw the array. 3×4	Draw a picture to model division.	Solve: $2 \times ? = 10$.	Split this array: 3×4
DOK Level 2 (These are questions where students have to use information, think about concepts and reason.) This is considered a more challenging problem than a level 1 problem.	Explain what an array is. Draw an array and explain what you are doing?	Mike had 24 apples. He split them evenly into 6 bags? How many apples were in each bag? In this word problem are we looking for how many are in each group or how many groups? How do you know? Explain your thinking	Solve: $3 \times ? = 12$ Model your thinking and explain your answer. What strategy did you use?	Split this array in 2 different ways and explain your thinking: 6×4
DOK Level 3 (These are questions where students have to reason, plan, justify, explain, and defend their thinking.)	Draw at least 3 different arrays for 12. Explain your thinking with numbers, words and pictures.	Write and solve a division word problem	Solve: $3 \times ? = 12$. Tell a word problem for this equation. Model the problem and defend your answer.	Make up your own problem. Split the array in 2 different ways. Explain your thinking. Defend your answer.

Adapted from Kaplinsky (https://robertkaplinsky.com/depth-knowledge-matrix-elementary-math/). A great resource for asking open questions is Marion Small's *Good Questions: Great ways to differentiate mathematics instruction in the standards-based classroom.* (2017).

Also, Robert Kaplinsky has done a great job in pushing our thinking forward with the Depth of Knowledge Matrices he created. The Kentucky Department of Education (2007) has a great document illustrating DOK Matrices.

Figure 5.64 Asking rigorous questions:

DOK 1	DOK 2	DOK 3
	At this level students explain their thinking.	**At this level students have to justify, defend and prove their thinking with objects, drawings and diagrams.**
What is the answer to ???

Can you model the number?

Can you model the problem?

Can you identify the answer that matches this equation?

How many hundreds, tens and ones are in this number? | How do you know that the equation is correct?

Can you pick the correct answer and explain why it is correct?

How can you model that problem?

What is another way to model that problem?

Can you model that on the . . . ???

Give me an example of a . . . type of problem . . .

Which answer is incorrect? Explain your thinking. | Can you prove that your answer is correct?

Prove that . . .

Defend your answer with words, pictures and numbers.

Show me how to solve that and explain what you are doing. Is there another way? Which way do you prefer and why? |

Key Points

♦ Building arrays
♦ Division
♦ Missing numbers
♦ Distributive property

Chapter Summary

Fluency is very important in third grade. It is much more than just knowing what the answer is to a problem. Students have to be able to contextualize problems. They should be able to tell stories about addition, subtraction, multiplication and division. They should have plenty of opportunities to work on missing numbers and make the connections between the operations. They should understand the properties. They should work with concrete manipulatives, do math sketches and work with symbols. This takes time across the year.

Reflection Questions

1. How are you currently doing fluency lessons?
2. Are you making sure that you do concrete, pictorial and abstract activities?
3. What do your students struggle with the most and what ideas are you taking away from this chapter that might inform your work around those struggles?

References

Baroody, J., Purpura, D., Eiland, M., & Reid, E., & Paliwal, V. (2016). Does fostering reasoning strategies for relatively difficult combinations promote transfer by k-3 students? *Journal of Educational Psychology, 108*(4).

Bay-Williams, J., & Kling, B. (2019). *Math fact fluency.* Reston, VA: ASCD.

Boaler, J. (2015). *Fluency without fear: Research evidence on the best ways to learn math facts.* Retrieved September 6, 2019 from www.youcubed.org/evidence/fluency-without-fear/Brownell, W. A. (1956, October). Meaning and skill—maintaining the balance. *Arithmetic Teacher, 3,* 129–136.

Brownell, W. A., & Chazal, C. B. (1935, September). The effects of premature drill in third-grade arithmetic. *Journal of Educational Research, 29,* 17–28.

Godfrey, C., & Stone, J. (2013). Mastering fact fluency: Are they game? *Teaching Children Mathematics, 20*(2), 96–101.

Henry, V., & Brown, R. (2008). First-grade basic facts: An investigation into teaching and learning of an accelerated, high-demand memorization standard. *Journal for Research in Mathematics Education, 30*(2), 1153–1183.

Kamii, C., Kirkland, L., & Lewis, B. (2001). Fluency in subtraction compared with addition. *Journal of Mathematical Behavior, 20,* 33–42.

Kentucky Department of Education. (2007). *Support materials for core content for assessment version 4.1 mathematics.* Retrieved January 15, 2017.

Mathematics Learning Study Committee, Center for Education, Division of Behavioral and Social Sciences and Education, National Research Council, Kilpatrick, J., Swafford, J., & Findell, B. (Eds.). (2001). *Adding it up: helping children learn mathematics.* Washington, DC: National Academy Press.

National Center for Education Evaluation and Regional Assistance. (2009). *Assisting students struggling with mathematics: Response to Intervention (RtI) for elementary and middle schools. 2009–4060.* Retrieved IES from http://ies.ed.gov/ncee and http://ies.ed.gov/ncee/wwc/publications/practiceguides/

National Council of Teachers of Mathematics. (2000). *Principles and standards for school mathematics.* Reston, VA: National Council of Teachers of Mathematics.

Newton, R. (2016). *Math running records.* New York: Routledge.

Newton, R., Record, A., & Mello, A. (2020). *Fluency doesn't just happen.* New York: Routledge.

Small, M. (2017). *Good questions: Great ways to differentiate math in the standards based classroom.* New York: Teachers College Press.

Thornton, C. (1978). Emphasizing thinking strategies in basic fact instruction. *Journal for Research in Mathematics Education, 9*(3), 214–225. Reston, VA: NCTM.

Van de Walle, J. A. (2007). *Elementary and middle school mathematics: Teaching developmentally.* Boston, MA: Pearson /Allyn and Bacon.

Webb, N. (2002). *An analysis of the alignment between mathematics standards and assessments for three states.* Paper presented at the annual meeting of the American Educational Research Association, New Orleans, LA.

6
Small Group Word Problem Lessons

It is important to teach about word problems in small guided math groups. Word problems have a specific learning trajectory as outlined in the *Cognitively Guided Instruction* work (Carpenter, Fennema, Franke, Levi, & Empson, 1999/2015). There are specific categories and levels of problems. Students should get an opportunity to explore solving various problems in various ways. This work should be scaffolded in the guided math group.

Every state has outlined the types of problems by grades that students should be working on. In the guided math group, teachers scaffold the learning so that students are working in their zone of proximal development towards the grade level standards. The reality is that some problems are more challenging than others. Also, even within categories, number ranges can vary and should be scaffolded.

We also look at several types of open problems, where students are much more responsible for actually creating the problems. We do 3 read protocol problems where students have to come up with the questions and then solve them. We look at numberless word problems that do what Brian Stuckus calls a "slow reveal" where the problem is slowly introduced to the students so that they can digest it in pieces (https://bstockus.wordpress.com/numberless-word-problems/). We also look at open problems, where there is context and then students make up the entire problem and solve it on a model.

DOI: 10.4324/9781003169543-6

Research Note 🔍

♦ Students have a tendency to "suspend sense-making" when they are solving problems. They don't stop to reason through the problem Schoenfeld, 1991; Verschaffel, Greer, & De Corte, 2000). We must find ways to slow the process down so they can think.

♦ Students develop a "compulsion to calculate" (Stacey & MacGregor, 1999) that can interfere with the development of the algebraic thinking that is needed to solve word problems (cited in https://cde.state.co.us/comath/word-problems-guide).

♦ Research consistently states that we should **never use key words**. From the beginning, teach students to reason about the context, not to depend on key words. See a great blog post that cites many articles on this: https://gfletchy.com/2015/01/12/teaching-key-words-forget-about-it/.

In this chapter we explore:

♦ Measurement problems
♦ Multiplication tile and tape diagram problems
♦ Elapsed time problems
♦ 3 read problems
♦ Picture prompts (see Figures 6.1 to 6.57)

Measurement Problems

Overview

Figure 6.1 Overview

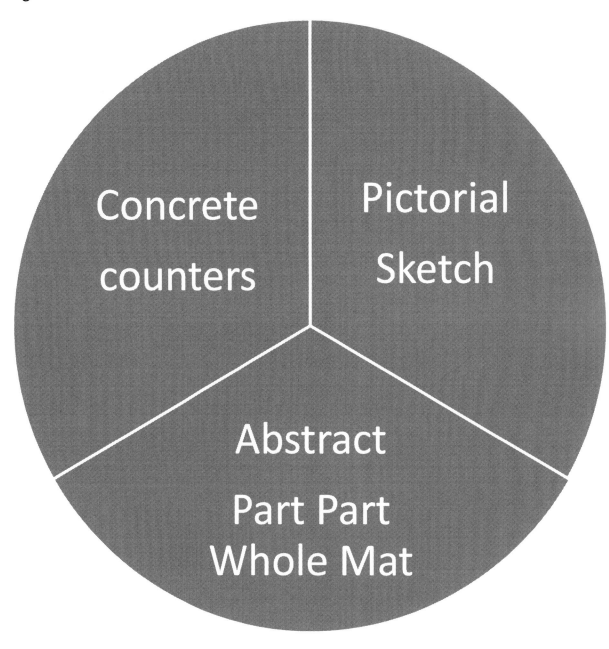

Figure 6.2 Planning Template

Measurement Word Problems

Big Idea: There are different types of word problems. **Enduring Understanding:** We can model problems in many ways. **Essential Question:** What are the ways to model word problems? **I can statement:** I can model measurement problems.	**Materials** • Tools: Measurement Cups • Templates: Measurement Cups • Cards • Crayons
Cycle of Engagement **Concrete:**  **Pictorial: Drawing**  **Abstract:** Sue poured some milk into the cake mix. Then, she poured 500 ml more. Now she has a liter. How much did she have in the beginning?	Vocabulary & Language Frames Beakers Measurement Cups Start Change End Liters Milliliters _____ started with _____. _____ got some more. Now there are _____.

Figure 6.3 Differentiated Lessons

Three Differentiated Lessons
In this series of lessons, students are working on measurement problems. Different state standards have different requirements. All third graders are expected to solve two-step problems. I have just given them a measurement context here. Students are working on developing this concept through concrete activities, pictorial activities and abstract activities. Everybody should do the cycle. Some students progress through it more quickly than others. Here are some things to think about as you do these lessons.

Emergent	On Grade Level	Above Grade Level
Review adding. As you introduce this to students, do a lot of work by acting it out and then doing it with manipulatives. Be sure to have students draw what they acted out and connect it to number models. Be sure that students are proficient with all the addition and subtraction word problem types.	The grade level standard is that students can act out, model, and explain word problems. So do lots of this work where students are modeling and explaining their thinking.	Have students do more work with multi-step, multidigit word problems.

 Looking for Misunderstandings and Common Errors

Measurement is a very tricky topic for students. Students need to have hands on experiences with it. Students need the concrete experiences with different types of measurement. Really they need to understand conceptually what we are doing. They should act out the problems at the small group table amidst conversation and discussion about the topic.

Concrete Lesson

Figure 6.4 Concrete Introduction

<table>
<tr><td colspan="2" align="center">Introduction of Concrete Explorations:
Open Measurement Problems</td></tr>
<tr><td>Launch</td><td>Teacher: Today we are going to do a measurement activity (make sure you send home letters about any allergies before you do this and get them signed by parents for participation).

Vocabulary: milliliters, liters, capacity, measure

Math talk: We used _____ ml.</td></tr>
<tr><td>Model</td><td>Today we are going to talk about making fruit punch. Grandma has 3 ingredients. She has some orange juice, some pineapple juice and some cranberry juice. She wants to make a half liter of punch. What could some possibilities for the recipe be?

Students taste test and work together to come up with a recipe for what the punch could be. They talk about what they like, what they don't like and what the strong flavor should be. They then try out the recipe at the table with the teacher asking questions.</td></tr>
<tr><td>Checking for Understanding</td><td>Teacher: Who can tell me about one of your recipes?

Maite: We tried 150 ml apple juice, 150 ml of orange juice and 150 ml of pineapple juice.

Ted: We liked it!</td></tr>
</table>

Record of Thinking

1st Try	2nd Try

Figure 6.5 Student Activity

	Concrete Student Activity
Guided Practice/ Checking for Understanding	The teacher passes out the problems. Students pull a card and act out their problems. The students each get a chance to share their problem and explain how they solved it.
	Maria: My problem is this:
	Luke drank 750 ml of water all day. How much could he have drank at different times?
	So, I looked at my measurement cup and I broke up 750 ml. I said that he drank 300 ml of water in the morning and 300 ml of water at lunch and 150 right before bed.
	Teacher: What did you notice while looking at the measuring cup?
	Maria: I noticed how much a liter is.
	Teacher: What are some other things that you all noticed.
	Hong: I looked at the measuring cup and the bottle of water to tell my story. It is interesting to think about the amount.
Set up for Independent Practice	**Teacher:** That is great! We are going to continue working with the measuring cups in the workstations and also do some drawings.

Figure 6.6 Lesson Close

Close
• What did we do today?
• What was the math we were practicing?
• How did we model the math?
• Was this easy or tricky?
• Turn to a partner and state one thing you learned today.

Figure 6.7 Start Unknown Problem Cards

Mike drank a liter of water during the day. What are the different amounts that he could have drank throughout the day?	Carla drank 200 ml of water in the morning and then some more in the afternoon. Altogether she drank 1000 ml. How much did she drink in the afternoon?
Ricky drank 500 ml of water in the morning and 500 ml of water in the afternoon. He drank some more in the evening. He drank a total of a liter and a half. How much did he drink in the evening?	Lucy drank 1200 ml of water. Mike drank a liter of water. Who drank more and how much more?
Mike drank 2 liters of water during the day. What are the different amounts that he could have drank throughout the day?	Carla drank 400 ml of water in the morning and then some more in the afternoon. She drank a total of 1.5 l of water. How much did she drink in the afternoon?
Ricky drank 500 ml of water in the morning and 500 ml of water in the afternoon. He drank some more in the evening. He drank a total of 2 liters. How much did he drink in the evening?	Lucy drank ½ a liter of water. Mike drank 780 ml of water. Who drank more and how much more?

Visual Lesson

Figure 6.8 Visual Introduction

Introduction to Visual Explorations

Launch	**Teacher:** Today we are going to work on solving pictorial measurement activities. Vocabulary: **add, start, word problem, count up, number sentence (equation), missing number, gram (g), kilogram (kl),** Math Talk: The mass is about ___ kilograms. The mass is about _____ grams.
Model	**Teacher:** Today we are going to talk about mass. I am going to show you some things and then ask you what do you notice and what do you wonder about their mass.

1 Gram	1 Kilogram
Paper clip **Piece of paper** **Penny Feather**	**A book** **6 apples**

Teacher: What do you notice about our things?

Ted: I noticed that grams are light and kilograms weigh more.

Teacher: Today you are going to take a walk around the room and then find and write down things that you would weigh in grams and kilograms. Here is your recording sheet. Sketch your object. When you come back be ready to defend your thinking.

Notes and Observations

Recording Sheet of things around the classroom

Grams	Kilograms

Checking for Understanding	*Students get up and walk around the room and write down different things either as being measured in grams or kilograms. Then they come back to talk about their observations and sketches*

Figure 6.9 Student Activity

	Visual Student Activity
Guided Practice/ Checking for Understanding	Everyone meets back at the table after about 5 minutes and they discuss their findings and their drawings. **Jamil:** I put a pencil as something we would weigh in grams and the desk as something we would weight in kilograms. The pencil is very light and the desk is very heavy compared to the pencil. **Recording Sheet of things around the classroom** | Grams	Kilograms
Pencil Crayon Paper Clip	Desk Chair Door | **Notes and Observations** Grams are light and kilograms are heavy. **Teacher:** Who agrees with him? **Grace:** I do. I put the crayon under grams and the chair under kilograms.
Set up for Independent Practice	*Teacher gives everybody a chance to discuss some of their observations and explain their thinking. After everyone has shared the lesson ends.* We are going to be talking more about this in the upcoming days. Are there any questions? What was interesting today? What was tricky?

Figure 6.10

Recording Sheet of things around the classroom

Grams	Kilograms

Notes and Observations

Figure 6.11 Lesson Close

Close

- What did we do today?
- What was the math we were practicing?
- How did we model the math?
- Was this easy or tricky?
- Turn to a partner and state one thing you learned today.

Abstract Lesson

Figure 6.12 Abstract Introduction

	Introduction to Abstract Explorations
Launch	**Teacher:** Today we are going to continue work on solving measurement word problems. **Vocabulary:** add, Start Unknown, word problem, count up, number sentence (equation), total **Math Talk:** My strategy is to _____. I modeled my thinking by _____. I know my answer is correct because _____.
Model	**Teacher:** I am going to give you some word problems, and we will reason them out with different models and tools. Here is one. *Mike drank some punch. Then, he drank 275 more milliliters of punch. All total he drank 750 ml of punch. How much did he drink in the beginning?* **Ted**: Well, 275 plus 25 is 300 plus 450 is 750. So he drank 475 ml in the beginning.
Checking for Understanding	**Teacher:** Any other thoughts? **Connie:** You could also subtract 275 from 750. And that would be 475. **Teacher:** Yes, we could do that. I am going to read the problem, and then you will illustrate it and show it to the group. We will take turns explaining our thinking. Here we go.

Figure 6.13 Student Activity

Abstract Student Activity	
Guided Practice/ Checking for Understanding	The teacher reads different problems. The children solve the problems however they want and then they solve them using different tools and models and show them and explain their thinking to the group. Each time, a different student explains how they solved the problem. how they solved it.
	Josephine explains: I used a part-part whole mat. The problem said Grandma Mary made some punch. Then, she added 500 more ml. Now she has 900 ml of punch. How much did she have in the beginning? So, I can count up from 500 to 900 and that would be 400.
	<table><tr><td colspan="2" align="center">900</td></tr><tr><td>?</td><td>500 ml</td></tr></table>
	Teacher: Yes.
	Everybody models the problems and show it on their part-part whole mat. Some students have the numbers in the wrong place and they erase and fix it. Teacher reminds everybody that it is ok to make mistakes because that means you are trying and when you keep trying you will get it.
	Teacher: We are going to be talking more about this in the upcoming days. Are there any questions? What was interesting today? What was tricky?
	Kelly: I think it is tricky to know where the numbers go. **Teacher:** Yes it can be tricky. Who can give us some ideas on how to work with the numbers?
	Jamal: You have to look at the total and that goes at the top. The other number is how many there were so that goes in this box. The missing number always goes wherever the part is that you are looking for.
Set up for Independent Practice	**Teacher:** Ok then. Everybody write down either one thing you learned or 1 question you have before you go to your workstations. .

Figure 6.14 Lesson Close

Close
• What did we do today?   • What was the math we were practicing?   • How did we model the math?   • Was this easy or tricky?   • Turn to a partner and share one thing you learned today.

Figure 6.15 Problem Solving Cards

? + 500ml = 1L	Luke made some punch. He then added 500 ml of cranberry juice. Now he has 1 liter of punch. How much did he have in the beginning?
? + 200 ml = 1L	Luke made some punch. He then added 200 ml of cranberry juice. Now he has 1 liter of punch. How much did he have in the beginning?
? + 440 ml = 790 ml	Luke made some punch. He then added 440 ml of cranberry juice. Now he has 790 ml of punch. How much did he make in the beginning?
? + 500 ml = 1L	Luke made some punch. He then added 500 ml of cranberry juice. Now he has 1 liter of punch. How much did he put in?

(Continued)

(Continued)

? + 200 ml = 500 ml	Luke made some punch. He then put 200 ml of cranberry juice in it. Now he has half a liter. How much did he make in the beginning?

Section Summary

Measurement problems can be very tricky. Students have to not only work on what is happening in the situation of the problem, but they also are working with understanding metric units of measure and in some states, customary units of measure as well in third grade. Start Unknown problems can be very tricky. The Add to Start Unknown problems should be scaffolded with base ten blocks and in part-part whole mats. The counters provide that physical contact so students can move them around to make sense of the problem. The part-part whole mat is a great abstract visual because students can see the numbers. Number lines and number grids are also great abstract visual scaffolds because students can see the numbers. Eventually you want students to be able to reason it out with just equations and/or mental math.

Modeling Multiplication Word Problems with Tiles and Tape/Strip Diagrams

Overview

Figure 6.16 Overview

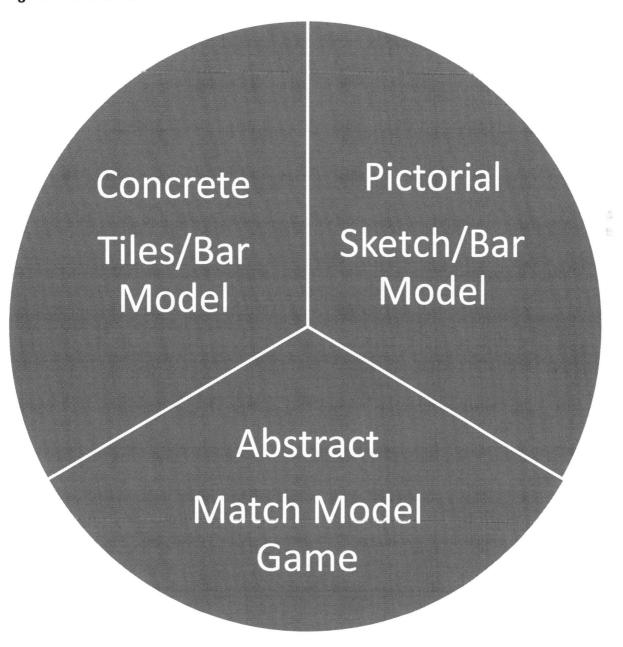

Figure 6.17 Planning Chart

Multiplicationo Problems with Bar/Tape/Strip Diagrams

Big Idea: There are different types of word problems.

Enduring Understanding: We can model multiplication problems in many ways including tape/strip diagrams.

Essential Question: What are the ways to model this type of problem?

I can statement: I can model multiplication problems with bar/tape/strip diagrams

Materials
- Tools: 1 inch tiles, paper
- Cards
- Crayons

Cycle of Engagement

Concrete:

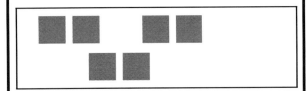

Pictorial: Drawing

Abstract: Bar/Tape/Strip diagram

?

2	2	2

Vocabulary & Language Frames

One inch tile model
Bar/ Strip/Tape Diagram

Figure 6.18 Differentiated Lessons

Three Differentiated Lessons
In this series of lessons, students are working on the concept of modeling multiplication word problems using tiles and bar/tape/strip diagrams. They are developing this concept through concrete activities, pictorial activities and abstract activities. Everybody should do the cycle. Some students progress through it more quickly than others. Here are some things to think about as you do these lessons.

Emergent	On Grade Level	Above Grade Level
Students need to understand one-step problems. Make sure that students understand the idea of problem solving, solving one way and checking another. Make sure that you as the teacher have scaffolded the problems.	The grade level standard is that students can model and solve multiplication and division word problems. So do lots of this work where students are modeling it and explaining it.	Extend the number range. Focus on multi-step problems not just two-step problems.

 Looking for Misunderstandings and Common Errors

Students have trouble modeling word problems. They need many opportunities to work with small numbers and manipulatives so they can visualize and model the problems and then sketch them and solve them.

Figure 6.19 Anchor Chart

Solving Multiplication Word Problems with Tape Diagrams

Jane and her 2 friends each have 2 rings. How many rings do they have altogether?

1 inch tile model

Math Sketch

? total rings

2	2	2

Jane   Friend 1   Friend 2

3 groups of 2

3 x 2 = 6

Concrete Lesson

Figure 6.20 Concrete Introduction

	Introduction to Concrete Explorations
Launch	**Teacher:** Today we are going to work on word problems. **Vocabulary: Product Factor Multiply Equal Groups. Arrays bar/strip/ tape diagram , represent** **Math Talk: The product is....**
Model	**(First the teacher reviews the vocabulary by asking the students to describe it and give examples)** **Teacher:** The bakery had 12 cupcakes. They put them in arrays. What could the array have looked like? Use your counters and work with a partner to show us. When you describe it use your math vocabulary. **Lucy:** Ted and me did 3 rows with 4 columns. That makes 12.

(Continued)

(Continued)

Checking for Understanding	**Sasha:** Luke and me did 2 rows and 6 columns. That makes 12.  **Teacher:** Excellent. Is there another way? **Ted:** Yes, they could have done 4 rows and 3 columns. **Luke:** Yes or 6 rows and 2 columns. **Teacher:** Ok. I am going to give each one of you your own problem. I want you to read it. Solve it. Be ready to share how you did it. I am going to watch you and if you need help, look at our anchor charts and of course you can ask me.

Figure 6.21 Student Activity

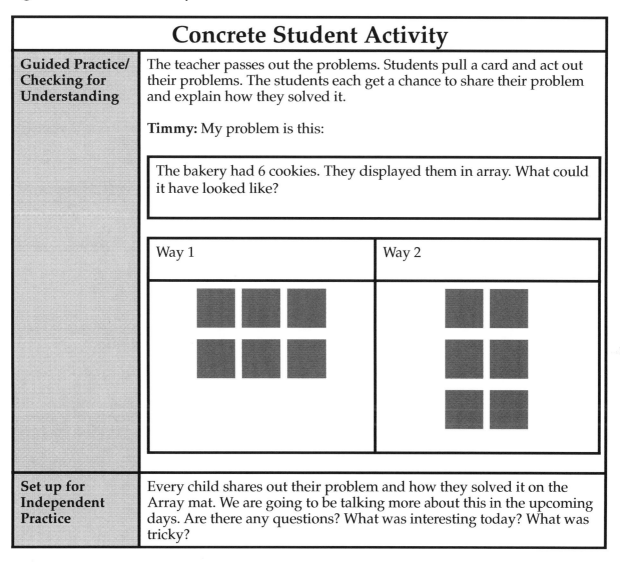

	Concrete Student Activity
Guided Practice/ Checking for Understanding	The teacher passes out the problems. Students pull a card and act out their problems. The students each get a chance to share their problem and explain how they solved it. **Timmy:** My problem is this: The bakery had 6 cookies. They displayed them in array. What could it have looked like? Way 1 / Way 2
Set up for Independent Practice	Every child shares out their problem and how they solved it on the Array mat. We are going to be talking more about this in the upcoming days. Are there any questions? What was interesting today? What was tricky?

Figure 6.22 Lesson Close

Close
• What did we do today? • What was the math we were practicing? • How did we model the math? • Was this easy or tricky? • Turn to a partner and state one thing you learned today.

Figure 6.23 Part-Part Whole Cards

The bakery had 4 cookies. They displayed them in an array. What could it have looked like?	The bakery had 6 cookies. They displayed them in an array. What could it have looked like?
The bakery had 8 cookies. They displayed them in an array. What could it have looked like?	The bakery had 10 cookies. They displayed them in an array. What could it have looked like?
The bakery had 24 cookies. They displayed them in an array. What could it have looked like?	The bakery had 12 cookies. They displayed them in an array. What could it have looked like?
The bakery had 16 cookies. They displayed them in an array. What could it have looked like?	The bakery had 20 cookies. They displayed them in an array. What could it have looked like?

Visual Lesson

Figure 6.24 Visual Introduction

Introduction to Visual Explorations

Launch	**Teacher:** Today we are going to continue to work on solving word problems and modeling them with a tape diagram. **Vocabulary:** multiplication, word problem, array, product, equal group, factor (**Math Talk:** The factors are ____ and ____. The product is _____.
Model	**The bakery had 6 rows of 2 cookies. How many cookies did they have altogether?** **Teacher:** How could we model this problem with a tape diagram? **Don:** Row 1. [2] Row 2 [2] Row 3 [2] Row 4 [2] Row 5. [2] Row 6 [2] } ? **Teacher:** Does everybody see this model? Who can explain it? Are the numbers in the right place? **Grace:** Yes. The product is 12. **Teacher:** What are the factors? **Tom:** 2 and 6. **Teacher:** Can somebody give me another problem where the product is 12?

(Continued)

Checking for Understanding	Lucas: We could say there were 2 rows with 6 cookies in each row. Teacher: Absolutely. What do we notice about that all those numbers? Maritza: They are the same. He just flipped it. So 2 × 6 is the same product as 6 × 2. Teacher: What would the tape diagram look like though? Would it be the same. Terrence: No. It would look like this: 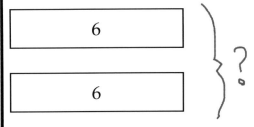 *This conversation continues with the students using tape diagrams to model their stories.*

Figure 6.25 Student Activity

Visual Student Activity

Guided Practice/ Checking for Understanding	The teacher passes out word problem cards. Students pull a card and model their problems. The students each get a chance to share their problem and explain how they solved it.
	Maria: My problem is this:
	There were 2 rows of apple trees on the farm. There were 4 trees in each row. How many apple trees were there altogether?
	Maria: Here is my model.
	4 4 } ?
	Brian: My problem said:
	The store had 5 baskets of oranges. There were 5 oranges in each basket. How many oranges were there altogether?
	? 5 5 5 5 5
	The store had 25 oranges. The product is 25. The factors are 5 and 5.
	Teacher: Does everybody see that? You all are doing really well modeling with the tape diagram.
Set up for Independent Practice	*Teacher gives everybody a chance to do and discuss a problem. After everyone has shared the lesson ends.* "We are going to be talking more about this in the upcoming days. Are there any questions? What was interesting today? What was tricky?"

Figure 6.26 Lesson Close

Close
• What did we do today? • What was the math we were practicing? • How did we model the math? • Was this easy or tricky? • Turn to a partner and state one thing you learned today.

Figure 6.27 Tape Diagram Cards

The store had 5 baskets. There were 5 balls in each basket. How many balls did the store have altogether?	The store had 5 cases of water. There were 6 bottles of water in each case. How many bottles of water did the store have in total?
The store had 4 baskets. There were 10 balls in each basket. How many balls did the store have altogether?	The store had 7 cases of water. There were 6 bottles of water in each case. How many bottles of water did the store have in total?
The store had 5 baskets. There were 10 balls in each basket. How many balls did the store have altogether?	The store had 10 cases of water. There were 6 bottles of water in each case. How many bottles of water did the store have in total?
The store had 5 baskets. There were 7 marbles in each basket. How many marbles did the store have altogether?	The store had 8 boxes of strawberries. There were 10 big strawberries in each box. What was the total amount of strawberries?
The store had 2 baskets. There were 7 balls in each basket. How many balls did the store have altogether?	The store had 4 boxes of bananas. There were 9 bananas in each box. How many bananas did they have altogether?

Abstract Lesson

Figure 6.28 Abstract Introduction

<table>
<tr>
<td colspan="2" align="center"><h2>Introduction to Abstract Explorations</h2></td>
</tr>
<tr>
<td>Launch</td>
<td>

Teacher: Today we are going to play a word problem match game. You will match the problem, the tape diagram and the equation.

Vocabulary: part-part whole, whole, part, word problem, count up, number sentence (equation)

Math Talk. The whole is _____. One part is _____. The other part is _____.

</td>
</tr>
<tr>
<td>Model</td>
<td>

Teacher: Today we are going to play a match game. We have to find the word problem, the part- part whole diagram and the number sentence that all match. There are 3 problems that are all mixed up in the bags. I am going to let you work with your partner to talk and discuss the problems and match them up. I am going to listen and ask you questions. Let's do 1 together.

?	
5	5

2 × 5 = 10

There were 2 boxes of apples. There were 5 apples in each box. How many apples were there altogether?

</td>
</tr>
<tr>
<td>Checking for Understanding</td>
<td>

Teacher: Does everybody see this model. Who can explain it?

Ted: Well we know that there were 2 boxes with 5 in each box and we are looking for the product so there is a question mark at the top.

Connie: The equation is 2 × 5 = 10.

Teacher: Ok, does everyone see how to play the match game. I will be watching you discuss the problems with your partners. Be sure you are sure because I am going to definitely ask you questions about the matches you make.

</td>
</tr>
</table>

Figure 6.29 Student Activity

Abstract Student Activity	
Guided Practice/ Checking for Understanding	The teacher watches the students as they work together to discuss and match the problems. **Teacher watches Leah and Tom.** How do you know this equation goes with the problem? **Leah:** Because it shows 4 boxes and we are looking for the total number of marbles. *(diagram: a bar labeled ? divided into 10, 10, 10, 10; below it 4 × 10 = 40; beside it the problem:)* Luke had 4 boxes. In each box he put 10 marbles. How many marbles did he have altogether?
Set up for Independent Practice	The teacher continues to watch the groups as they work on matching their problems. When everyone has finished the teacher asks the students to explain their thinking. She also asks them what was easy and what was tricky.

Figure 6.30 Lesson Close

Close
• What did we do today? • What was the math we were practicing? • How did we model the math? • Was this easy or tricky? • Turn to a partner and state one thing you learned today.

Figure 6.31 Word problem cards

	?	
2		2

2 × 2 = ?

Luke had 2 boxes. He put 2 cars in each box. How many cars did he have altogether?

	?	
4		4

4 × 4 = ?

Maria had 2 boxes. She put 4 rings in each box. How many rings did she have altogether?

	?	
7		7

2 × 7 = ?

Hong had 2 boxes. He put 7 marbles in each box. How many marbles does he have altogether?

2	2	2	2

4 × 2 = ?

Luke had 4 boxes. He put 2 cars in each box. How many cars did he have altogether?

		?		
4	4	4	4

4 × 4 = ?

Maria had 4 boxes. She put 4 rings in each box. How many rings did she have altogether?

(Continued)

(Continued)

			?			
2	2	2	2	2	2	2

Hong had 7 boxes. He put 2 marbles in each box. How many marbles does he have altogether?

$$7 \times 2 = ?$$

Section Summary

In this section we have talked about solving multiplication problems with a focus on using tiles and tape diagrams. In most state standards, students should be introduced to tape diagrams in the second grade. Sometimes, this doesn't happen. In either case, it is good to start with 1-inch tiles as the scaffold for doing this concretely and then drawing out what they did. They could also use Cuisenaire ^{tm} rods to do this. The next step is to have the students draw what they built. This cycle of concrete, pictorial to abstract is a great cycle to build student confidence about being able to model their thinking with tape diagrams.

Elapsed Time Word Problems

Overview

Figure 6.32 Overview

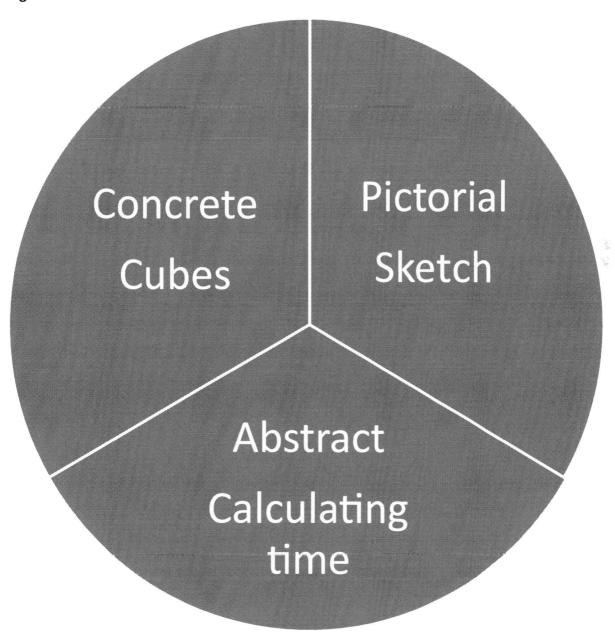

Figure 6.33 Planning Template

Elapsed Time Word Problems	
Big Idea: There are different types of elapsed time word problems. The big idea is for students to understand how we measure time. **Enduring Understanding**: We can model problems in many ways. **Essential Question**: What are the ways to model elapsed time problems? **I can statement**: I can model elapsed time word problems.	**Materials** • Tools: Cubes • Templates: Ten Frame • Cards • Crayons
Cycle of Engagement **Concrete:**  **Pictorial: Drawing** 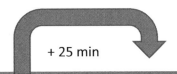 + 25 min 5:10 5:35 **Abstract: Mental Calculations** 10 + 25 = 35	**Vocabulary & Language Frames** • Count Up • Count Back • Minutes • Hours • Hands • Start time • End time • Elapsed Time

Figure 6.34 Differentiated Lessons

Three Differentiated Lessons

In this series of lessons, students are working on elapsed time problems. They are developing this concept through concrete activities, pictorial activities and abstract activities. Everybody should do the cycle. Some students progress through it more quickly than others. Here are some things to think about as you do these lessons.

Below Grade Level	On Grade Level	Above Grade Level
Review adding and subtracting. As you introduce this to students, do a lot of work by acting it out and then doing it with manipulatives. Review the first grade standards of telling time by the half hour. Review the second grade standards of telling time by 5 minute intervals.	Students should work with manipulatives such as the beaded number line before they jump into working with an abstract number line. Braining camp also has a great virtual clock!	Extend the number range telling time across hours.

 Looking for Misunderstandings and Common Errors

Elapsed time problems are tricky. In addition to the beaded number line, I like to teach them with the cubes going around so the students can physically count the minutes first. Then I like to do it with an illustrated clock before they move onto a number line diagram.

Figure 6.35 Anchor Chart

Solving Elapsed Time Problems

Concrete

Pictorial: Drawing

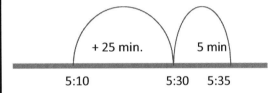

Abstract: Mental Calculations

10 + 20 + 5 = 35

Concrete Lesson

Figure 6.36 Concrete Introduction

Introduction to Concrete Explorations

Launch	**Teacher:** Today we are going to work on telling time problems. We will use our beaded number lines of 60 beads to help us. **Vocabulary: elapsed time Minutes Hours Ruler measure** **Math Talk: ____ minutes passed** **Students use the beaded number line.**
Model	**Part 1: What do we know?** **Part 2: What's next?** **Solution:** **Teacher:** Listen to this problem. Kiyana left her house at 3:05. She came back 15 minutes later. What time did she get back? **Katie:** I counted it around the clock.

(Continued)

(Continued)

Checking for Understanding	**Part 1: What do we know?** We know she left at 3:05.
	Part 2: What's next? She came back in 15 minutes.
	Solution: It is 3:20. **Teacher:** Ok. Does everybody see what Katie did? Does it make sense? *Here's another problem:* *Michael left his house at 4:10. He came back 20 minutes later. How long was he gone?* **Teacher:** Ok. Who can explain a way to do it? **Ellie:** I just added 10 minutes and 10 minutes and I got 30 minutes. He came back at 4:30. **Teacher:** Who agrees and why? **Yessenia:** I agree. I counted up on my fingers….10, 20 and then 30. *Teacher reads 2 more problems that the group discusses.* **Teacher:** Ok. I am going to give each one of you your own problem. I want you to read it. Solve it. Be ready to share how you did it. I am going to watch you and if you need help, look at our anchor charts and of course you can ask me.

Figure 6.37 Student Activity

	Student Activity
Guided Practice/ Checking for Understanding	The teacher passes out the problems. Students pull a card and act out their problems with clock templates. The students each get a chance to share their problem and explain how they solved it. **Teacher:** Remy explain your thinking to us. **Remy:** My problem was: Tom left his house at 3:07 and he came back 20 minutes later. So I added 20 + 7 and I got 3:27.
Set up for Independent Practice	Every child shares out their problem and how they solved it on the clock templates. We are going to be talking more about this in the upcoming days. Are there any questions? What was interesting today? What was tricky?

Figure 6.38 Lesson Close

Close
• What did we do today?   • What was the math we were practicing?   • How did we model the math?   • Was this easy or tricky?   • Turn to a partner and state one thing you learned today.

Figure 6.39 Elapsed Time Problems

Kelly left her house at 3:10. She came back at 3:50. How long was she gone?	Sue left her house at 2:20. She was gone 20 minutes. What time did she return?
Marta left her house at 12:12. She came back at 12:20. How long was she gone?	Kiyana left her house at 5:50. She was gone 10 minutes. What time did she return?
Hong left his house at 7:08. He came back at 7:40. How long was he gone?	Bill left his house at 1:20. He was gone 30 minutes. What time did he return?

Visual Lesson

Figure 6.40 Visual Introduction

	Introduction to Visual Explorations
Launch	**Teacher:** Today we are going to work more on elapsed time problems. We are going to use a clock to look at the elapsed **Vocabulary: elapsed time, ruler, minutes, hours, hands,** **Teacher: Let's look at this clock.**
Model	 **Teacher**: Here is the problem: Melissa left her house at 3:05 and she came back at 3:25. How long was she gone? How can I solve that? **Tom:** We could skip count, 5,10,15,20 so she was gone 20 minutes.
Checking for Understanding	**Teacher:** Yes, could you model it with the clock too? **Jose:** Yes, start here (he points to 5 after) and counts by 5's. **Teacher:** Excellent work. How do you know you are correct? **Tom:** We could count all the lines between 5 and 25. **Teacher:** Yes we could do that too. Today I am going to let you each pick problems and solve them with a partner and then share your thinking with the group.

Figure 6.41 Student Activity

Visual Student Activity

Guided Practice/ Checking for Understanding	The teacher passes out word problem cards. Students pull a card and tell their problems. The students each get a chance to share their problem and explain how they solved it. They use the clock model to scaffold their thinking. **Maria:** Our problem was this: **Part 1: Masey left her house at 2:02. She came back at 2:12. How long was she gone?** **Way 1 with a model:** We counted from 2 minutes after to 12 minutes after. We marked it on the clock. It was 10 minutes. **Way 2 with numbers** We know that 2 plus 10 is 12 so the answer is 10 minutes.
Set up for Independent Practice	*Teacher gives everybody a chance to do and discuss a problem. After everyone has shared the lesson ends.* We are going to be talking more about this in the upcoming days. Are there any questions? What was interesting today? What was tricky?

Figure 6.42 Elapsed Time Word Problem Cards

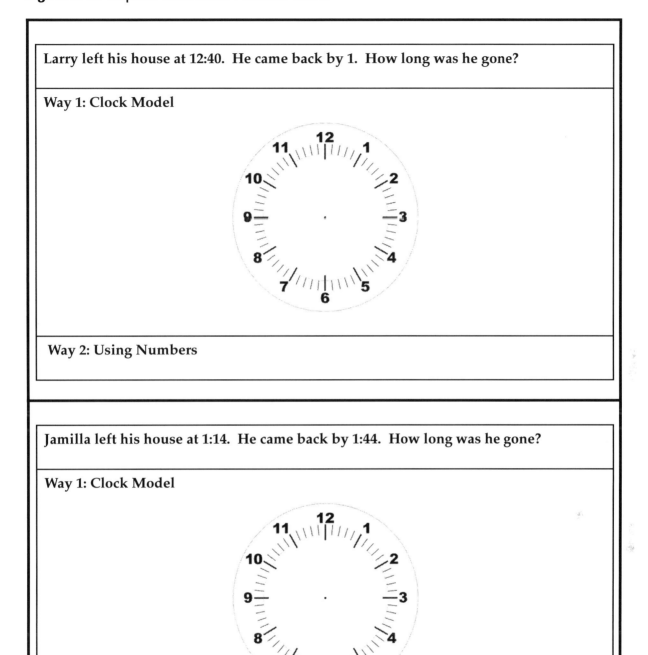

Larry left his house at 12:40. He came back by 1. How long was he gone?

Way 1: Clock Model

Way 2: Using Numbers

Jamilla left his house at 1:14. He came back by 1:44. How long was he gone?

Way 1: Clock Model

Way 2: Using Numbers

(Continued)

(Continued)

Lisa left her house at 12:00. She came back by 1. How long was she gone?

Way 1: Clock Model

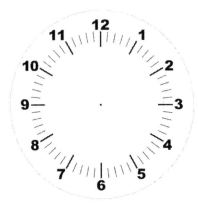

Way 2: Using Numbers

Mike left his house at 2:17. He came back by 2:29. How long was he gone?

Way 1: Clock Model

Way 2: Using Numbers

Krista left her house at _____. She came back by _____. How long was she gone?

Way 1: Clock Model

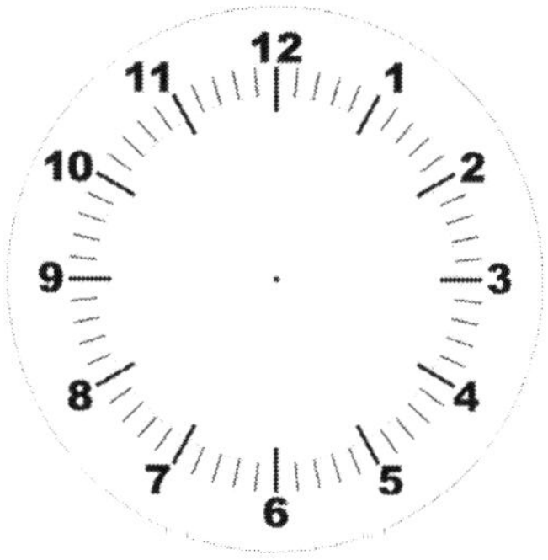

Way 2: Using Numbers

Miguel left his house at _____. He came back by _____. How long was he gone?

Way 1: Clock Model

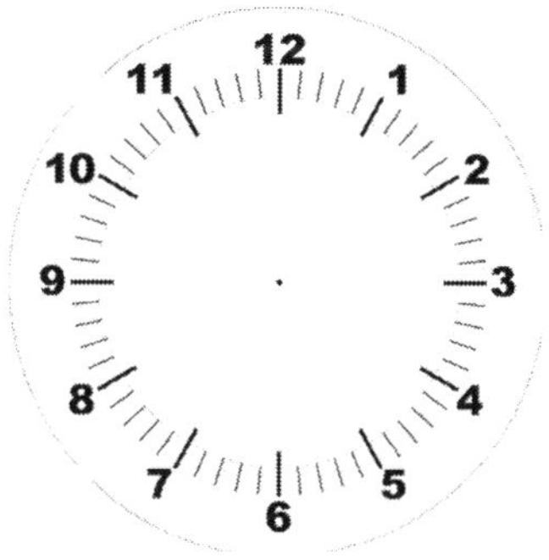

Way 2: Using Numbers

Figure 6.43 Lesson Close

Close

- What did we do today?
- What was the math we were practicing?
- How did we model the math?
- Was this easy or tricky?
- Turn to a partner and state one thing you learned today.

Abstract Lesson

Figure 6.44 Abstract Introduction

	Introduction to Abstract Explorations	
Launch	**Teacher:** Today we are going to continue to work solving elapsed time problems. Let's look at our math talk chart: **Vocabulary:** elapsed time, ruler, minutes, hours, hands, **Math Talk:** My strategy was _____. My model was _____.	
Model	**Teacher:** Lucy left her house at 3:07. She came back at 3:25. How long was she gone? Let's think about this together? How could we model the elapsed time on our number line? **Joe:** We could look at the 5 and then think about where 7 is and then jump to 10. Then from 10 we could jump to 25. Add up the amounts like we do on the open number line.	
Checking for Understanding	**Ted:** I jumped from 7 to 10. Then I jumped from 10 to 20 and then from 20 to 25. So I got 3 + 10 + 5 which is 18. **Miki:** I jumped from 7 to 10 and then I counted by 5's. I went 5,10,15 + 3 which was 18. **Teacher:** Ok, so just like with the open number line, we can jump different ways? Tell me why you all jumped from 7 to 10 first. **Joe:** Because in whole group we talked about getting to the tens because they are friendly numbers. **Miki:** They make it easier to count the time. **Teacher:** Ok, I am going to give each one of you your own problem and I want you to read your problem and then decide which way you are going to model your problem. Each person is going to get a chance to do one and explain their thinking	

Figure 6.45 Student Activity

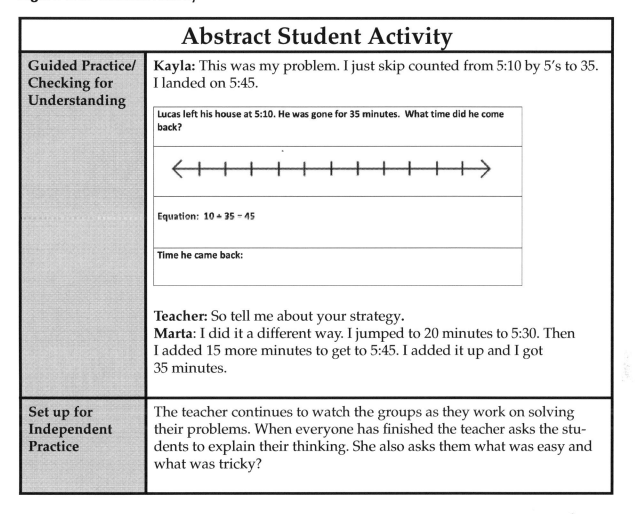

Abstract Student Activity

Guided Practice/ Checking for Understanding	**Kayla:** This was my problem. I just skip counted from 5:10 by 5's to 35. I landed on 5:45.
	<table><tr><td>Lucas left his house at 5:10. He was gone for 35 minutes. What time did he come back?</td></tr><tr><td>⟵—+—+—+—+—+—+—+—+—+—+—⟶</td></tr><tr><td>Equation: 10 + 35 = 45</td></tr><tr><td>Time he came back:</td></tr></table>
	Teacher: So tell me about your strategy. **Marta:** I did it a different way. I jumped to 20 minutes to 5:30. Then I added 15 more minutes to get to 5:45. I added it up and I got 35 minutes.
Set up for Independent Practice	The teacher continues to watch the groups as they work on solving their problems. When everyone has finished the teacher asks the students to explain their thinking. She also asks them what was easy and what was tricky?

Figure 6.46 Lesson Close

Close

- What did we do today?
- What was the math we were practicing?
- How did we model the math?
- Was this easy or tricky?
- Turn to a partner and state one thing you learned today.

Figure 6.47 Word Problem Cards

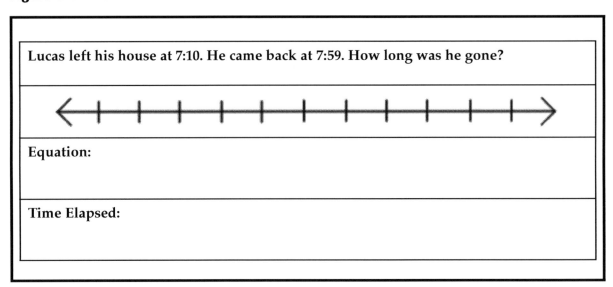

Lucas left his house at 7:10. He came back at 7:59. How long was he gone?

Equation:

Time Elapsed:

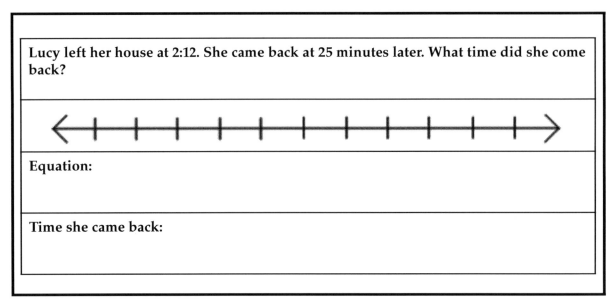

Lucy left her house at 2:12. She came back at 25 minutes later. What time did she come back?

Equation:

Time she came back:

Letecia left her house. She came back at 6:43. She was gone for 20 minutes. What time did she leave?

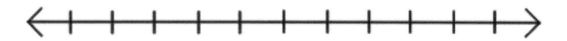

Equation:

Start Time:

Larry left his house at 9:19 a.m. He came back at 29 minutes later. What time did he come back?

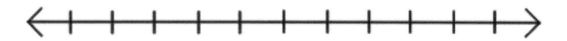

Equation:

End Time:

(Continued)

(Continued)

Luke left his house at. He came back at 4:57. He was gone for 30 minutes. What time did he leave his house?

←――→

Equation:

End Time:

Lilly left her house at 1:01. She came back at 1:25. How long was she gone?

←――→

Equation:

Time Elapsed:

Tell a story about this time line diagram.

| 1:45 | 1:55 | 2:00 | 2:05 |

Equation:

Time Elapsed:

Section Summary

Students have a great deal of trouble with elapsed time problems. Using various scaffolds up until they can draw a number line diagram to solve the problems takes time. Small groups are a great space to explore modeling these problems in different ways. In this section we looked at the different types of elapsed time problems. It is important to work on all the different types of problems and to have students explain their strategies for solving them.

3 Read Problems

Figure 6.48 3 Read Problem Chart

<table>
<tr><td colspan="2" align="center"><h2>3 Read Problems</h2></td></tr>
<tr>
<td>Big Idea: We can use different strategies and models to solve word problems.

Enduring Understanding: We can model problems in many ways.

Essential Question: What are the ways to model this type of problem?

I Can Statement: I can use tools to model my thinking.</td>
<td>Materials
♦ Tools: cubes
♦ Templates: ten frame
♦ Cards
♦ Crayons</td>
</tr>
<tr>
<td rowspan="2">Cycle of Engagement

Concrete-Pictorial-Abstract

In this type of problem, the class chorally reads the problem 3 times. The first time the class reads the problem, they focus on what is happening in the problem. The second time, they focus on what the numbers mean. The third time, they focus on asking questions about the problem.</td>
<td>Vocabulary and Language Frames

Strategies

Models

Tools</td>
</tr>
<tr>
<td>Mathematical Processes/Practices

Problem Solving

Reasoning

Modeling

Tools</td>
</tr>
</table>

Figure 6.49 3 Read Word Problem

3 Read Word Problem

We can read a problem 3 times.

The first time, we read it and think about the situation.

What is the story about? Who is in it? What is happening?

The second time, we read it and think about the numbers.

What are the numbers? What do they mean? What might we do with those numbers in this situation?

The third time, we read it and think about what questions we could ask.

What do we notice in this story? What do we wonder? What do we want to ask about this story?

The Jones family went on vacation. They drove 125 miles on Monday. They drove 250 miles on Tuesday. They drove 120 miles on Wednesday.

First Read: What is this story about? It is about a family who went on vacation.

Second Read: What do the numbers mean? They tell us how far they drove. On Monday they drove 125 miles. On Tuesday they drove 250 miles, and on Wednesday they drove 120 miles.

Third Read: What could we ask about this story?

How far did they drive altogether?

How much farther did they drive on Monday than on Wednesday?

How many fewer miles did they drive on Wednesday than they drove on Tuesday?

Figure 6.50 3 Read Word Problems

	### *3 Read Word Problems Lesson*
Launch	**Teacher:** Today we are going to work on word problems. We are going to do a 3 read, like the ones we do in whole group. **Vocabulary: model, strategy,** **Math Talk: The whole is _____. One part is _____. The other part is**
Model	*Story: The bakery made several cookies. They made 96 chocolate chip, 48 peanut butter and 24 lemon ones.* *First Read: What is this story about?* *It is about the bakery. They have 3 different types of cookies.* *Second Read: What do the numbers mean?* *They have 96 chocolate chip cookies, 48 peanut butter cookies and 24 lemon ones.* *Third Read: What could we ask about this story?* *How many cookies were there altogether?* *How many cookies more chocolate chip cookies did they have than peanut butter ones?* *How many fewer lemon cookies do they have than chocolate chip cookies?*

(Continued)

(Continued)

| **Checking for Understanding** | *Teacher:* Ok, pick 2 questions and answer them. We will come back in a few minutes to discuss them…. Who answered question 1? Tell us your strategy and show us a model of your thinking. |

Timothy: I did how many do they have altogether? I modeled it in a part-part whole diagram. My strategy was to add the tens and then the ones.

?		
96	48	24

$90 + 40 + 20 = 150$
$6 + 8 + 4 = 18$
$150 + 18 = 168$

Teacher: Ok, who did question 2?
Eric: I did how many more chocolate chip cookies than peanut butter ones. I used the hundred grid. I slide down to 98 which is 50 more but then I subtracted 2 because I had added 2 too many. So I got 48 as the answer.

1	2	3	4	5	6	7	8	9	10
11	12	13	14	15	16	17	18	19	20
21	22	23	24	25	26	27	28	29	30
31	32	33	34	35	36	37	38	39	40
41	42	43	44	45	46	47	48	49	50
51	52	53	54	55	56	57	58	59	60
61	62	63	64	65	66	67	68	69	70
71	72	73	74	75	76	77	78	79	80
81	82	83	84	85	86	87	88	89	90
91	92	93	94	95	(96)	97	(98)	99	100

Students continue to share their thinking with the group. When they are done the teacher facilitates a conversation about what the math was for the day and then what students thought was easy and what they thought was tricky.

Figure 6.51 Lesson Close

Close
• What did we do today? • What was the math we were practicing? • Was this easy or tricky? • Turn to a partner and state one thing you've learned today.

Figure 6.52 Read Cards

The teacher had 70 pencils. 15 were blue and 14 were green, and the rest were yellow.	Terri biked 2 miles for 3 days. Mary biked 3 miles for 2 days.
Marta had 16 red marbles, 29 orange marbles and 45 blue marbles.	The store had 24 red apples, 37 green apples and 59 yellow apples.
The jewelry store had 224 gold rings and 349 silver rings.	Grandma made fruit punch. She used 500 ml of apple juice, 250 ml of orange juice and 750 ml of pineapple juice.
The bakery had 5 boxes of chocolate cupcakes with 5 cupcakes in each box. It also had 3 boxes of lemon cupcakes with 4 in each box.	The toy store had 1000 marbles. They had 324 rainbow marbles, they had 450 jumbo marbles, and the rest were mini marbles.

Picture Prompt Problems

Figure 6.53 Picture Prompt Word Problems Chart

Picture Prompt Word Problems

Big Idea: Word problems are a part of our everyday lives.	**Materials** • Tools: Cubes • Templates: Ten Frame • Cards • Crayons
Enduring Understanding: We can model problems in many ways. There are many different strategies to solve them. **Essential Question:** What are the ways to model problems? **I can statement:** I can model problems.	**Questions** • What is your strategy? • What is your model? • Why does that work? • How can you show that?

Cycle of Engagement

Concrete:

Pictorial: Drawing

Abstract: Equations

$2 + m = 8$

$2 + 6 = 8$

Vocabulary & Language Frames

Add, subtract, take away, sum, difference

My strategy was …

My model was …

Math Processes/Practices
• **Problem Solving**
• **Reasoning**
• **Models**
• **Tools**

Figure 6.54 Picture Prompt Word Problem Lesson

	Picture Prompt Word Problems
Launch	**Teacher:** Today we are going to work on word problems using picture prompts. **Vocabulary: model, strategy,** **Math Talk: The whole is _____. One part is _____. The other part is**
Model	**Teacher:** Today we are going to look at pictures and tell word problems. Let's think about some word problems for this picture. 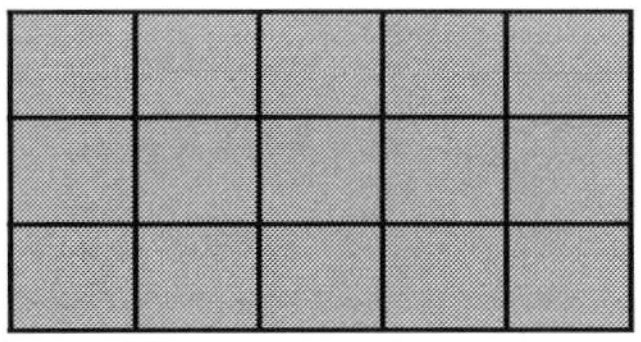 **Luke:** The candy bar had 3 rows and 5 columns. How many pieces of candy can you get? **Teacher:** Ok, that works! What's the product? **Marta:** 15 pieces. You could say: Kelly gave her sister 2 rows of her candy bar. How many pieces did she get? **Kelly:** 2×5 is 10 pieces.
Checking for Understanding	**Teacher:** Ok. Who's next? The teacher goes around the circle and everyone gets a chance to share their stories.

(Continued)

(Continued)

Guided Practice/ Checking for Understanding	**Teacher:** Who has another story? **Lara:** Marta gave her sister 3 columns of her candy bar. How much did she give her sister? **Marcos:** 3×3 is 9.
Set up for Independent Practice	The teacher goes around and everyone shares. When they done, they wrap up and students go to workstations.

Figure 6.55 Open Word Problems

<table>
<tr>
<td colspan="2" align="center"><h1>Open Word Problems Lesson
I can solve word problems.</h1></td>
</tr>
<tr>
<td>Launch</td>
<td>

Teacher: Today we are going to work on word problems.

Vocabulary: model, strategy, tool, sum, difference, addend,

Math Talk:
My strategy was ....
My model was .....
I know I am correct because...

</td>
</tr>
<tr>
<td>Model</td>
<td>

Teacher: The answer is 12 strawberries. What is the question? (Tell a multiplication or division word problem).

Terry: I know. There were 3 baskets and in each basket there were 4 strawberries. How many strawberries are there?

Kayla: I could say there were 2 baskets and 6 strawberries in each basket.
Teacher: Absolutely. All of these work. Can you both draw a model of what you said.

Teacher: Who can think of a division one with this quotient.

Kayla: Ok, I got one. Maite had a box of 24 strawberries. She shared it with her sister. How many did each person get?

Maite: 12

Joe: It's hard to think of division problems with 12 as the quotient.

Teacher: What might help us? (Students think out loud)....
 Let's think about how a table might help? How are multiplication and division related?

</td>
</tr>
</table>

(Continued)

(Continued)

	$2 \times 12 = 24$ $3 \times 12 = 36$ $4 \times 12 = 48$ $5 \times 12 = 60$ $6 \times 12 = 60$ $7 \times 12 = 84$ $8 \times 12 = 96$ **Taylor:** Well like we could say there were 36 strawberries and they were put into 3 boxes. How many were in each box?	
Checking for Understanding	**Teacher:** Yes because we can see here if the quotient is 12 then we are working with the two other numbers…. So for example, we could say the bakery had 48 strawberries and they put 4 in a box. How many boxes did they have? **Joe:** 12	
Guided Practice/ Checking for Understanding	**Teacher:** Who has another division problem? **Jamal:** The bakery had 24 strawberries. They put them in 2 in a box. How many boxes did they use? **Carol:** 12	
Set up for Independent Practice	*The students continue telling stories where the answer is 12. They focus on looking at the pattern. After they finish, the teacher asks them what they were doing and if it was easy or tricky. Then, the students are released back to continue their menu work.*	

Section Summary

It is important to do open questions with students where they have to contextualize numbers. This is part of the mathematical practices and processes (CCSSM, 2010; NCTM, 2000). We want students to be able to reason about numbers. We want students to be able to tell stories and not only solve them. Giving them rich structures to do that is vital.

Depth of Knowledge

Depth of Knowledge is a framework that encourages us to ask questions that require that students think, reason, explain, defend and justify their thinking (Webb, 2002). Here is a snapshot of what that can look like in terms of word problem work.

Figure 6.56 DOK Activities

	What are different strategies and models that we can use to solve measurement problems?	What are different strategies and models to model multiplication problems with tiles and tape diagrams?	What are different strategies and models that we can use to solve elapsed time problems?
DOK Level 1 (These are questions where students are required to simply recall/reproduce an answer/do a procedure.)	Solve. Write a set-up equation (with a symbol for the unknown) and a solution equation. Grandma used 240 ml of apple juice, 367 ml of orange juice and 199 ml of pineapple juice, in her fruit punch. How much fruit punch did she make?	Solve with manipulatives. Write the equation. The bakery had a display of donuts. They had 3 rows with 5 donuts in each row. How many donuts did they have altogether?	Sue left her house at 2:10. She came back at 2: 55. How long was she gone?
DOK Level 2 (These are questions where students have to use information, think about concepts and reason.) This is considered a more challenging problem than a level 1 problem.	Solve and model in two different ways. Explain your thinking. Grandma made fruit punch. She used 240 ml of apple juice, 367 ml of orange juice and the rest was pineapple juice. How much orange juice did she use?	Solve with a math sketch. Write the set-up equation and the solution equation. Explain your thinking. The bakery had a display of donuts. They had ___ rows with ___ donuts in each row. How many donuts did they have altogether?	Solve the problem with a model and an equation. Sue left her house at 2:10. She came back at _____. How long was she gone?
DOK Level 3 (These are questions where students have to reason, plan, explain, justify and defend their thinking.)	Solve. Grandma made some fruit punch. She used apple, orange and pineapple juice. She made 1 liter of punch altogether. What are some possible combinations of the juice that she could have made? Defend your answer. Prove that it is correct by solving one way and checking another.	Solve. The answer is 12. Make up an array problem. Write the set-up equation and the solution equation. Defend your answer. Prove that it is correct by solving one way and checking another.	Marcus was gone for 25 minutes. When could he have left and when could he have come back? Make up a problem and solve it on the number line. Defend your thinking. Prove that you are correct.

A great resource for asking open questions is Marion Small's *Good Questions: Great ways to differentiate mathematics instruction in the standards-based classroom*. (2017).

Also, Robert Kaplinsky has done a great job in pushing our thinking forward with the Depth of Knowledge Matrices he created. (**https://robertkaplinsky.com/depth-knowledge-matrix-elementary-math/**). Kentucky Math Department of Education (2007) has an excellent DOK Math Matrix Document as well.

Figure 6.57 Asking rigorous questions:

DOK 1	DOK 2	DOK 3
	At this level students explain their thinking.	**At this level students have to justify, defend and prove their thinking with objects, drawings and diagrams.**
What is the answer to ??? Can you model the problem? Can you identify the answer that matches this equation?	How do you know that the equation is correct? Can you pick the correct answer and explain why it is correct? How can you model that problem in more than one way? What is another way to model that problem? Can you model that on the . . . ??? Give me an example of a . . . type of problem . . . Which answer is incorrect? Explain your thinking.	Can you prove that your answer is correct? Prove that . . . Defend your answer. Show me how to solve that and explain what you are doing.

Key Points

♦ Measurement problems
♦ Multiplication tile and tape diagram problems
♦ Elapsed time problems
♦ 3 read problems
♦ Picture prompts

Chapter Summary

It is important to work with students in small guided math groups focusing on word problems. Word problems have a learning trajectory (Carpenter et al., 1999/2015). Most states have outlined the word problem types that each grade level is responsible for in their standards. So, in a guided math group, the goal is to work with students around the word problem types that they are learning.

Students are usually working at different levels of complexity when learning word problems. They are scaffolded into a hierarchy that goes from easy to challenging. By third grade, students dive deep into the six types of multiplication and division word problems, as well as measurement problems. Measurement is often difficult for students, and that is why it is so important to give students an opportunity to work in small groups to experience the math, to do the measurements.

The small group discussion should reference the whole group problem solving work. The focus should be on getting students to think about the context and the numbers, to reason about the problem and use visual representations and tools to unpack it. Students should have to write an equation with a symbol for the unknown and solve one way and check another. Problem solving should be done throughout the year, in different parts of math workshop, during the introduction, in math workstations, sometimes in guided math groups and sometimes for homework.

Reflection Questions

1. How are you currently teaching word problem lessons?
2. Are you making sure that you do concrete, pictorial and abstract activities?
3. What do your students struggle with the most and what ideas are you taking away from this chapter that might inform your work?

References

Carpenter, T. P., Fennema, E., Franke, M. L., Levi, L., & Empson, S. B. (2015). *Children's mathematics: Cognitively guided instruction*. NH: Heinemann.

Common Core State Standards Mathematical Practices. (2010). Retrieved January 15, 2021 from http://www.corestandards.org/Math/Practice/

Kentucky Department of Education. (2007). *Support materials for core content for assessment version 4.1 mathematics*. Retrieved January 15, 2017.

NCTM. (2000). *Principles and standards for school mathematics*. Reston, VA: NCTM.

Schoenfeld, A. H. (1991). On mathematics as sense-making: An informal attack on the unfortunate divorce of formal and informal mathematics. In J. F. Voss, D. N. Perkins, & J. W. Segal (Eds.), *Informal reasoning and education* (pp. 311–343). Hillsdale, NJ: Lawrence Erlbaum Associates.

Small, M. (2017). *Good questions: Great ways to differentiate math in the standards based classroom*. New York: Teachers College Press.

Stacey, K., & MacGregor, M. (1999). Learning the algebraic method of solving problems. *The Journal of Mathematical Behavior, 18*(2), 149–167. https://doi.org/10.1016/S0732-3123(99)00026-7

Verschaffel, L., Greer, B., & De Corte, E. (2000). *Making sense of word problems*. Lisse, The Netherlands: Swets & Zeitlinger.

Webb, N. (2002). *An analysis of the alignment between mathematics standards and assessments for three states*. Paper presented at the annual meeting of the American Educational Research Association, New Orleans, LA.

7

Place Value Guided Math Lessons

In most states, in third grade there are only three place value standards. Students have to learn how to flexibly and confidently work with multi-digit numbers up to 10,000. They also have to learn how to round numbers and multiply multiples of 10 by single digit numbers. However, place value is the glue that holds it all together. In third grade one of the things that you want to do is really continue working on the second-grade standards so that students can become confident and proficient in the concepts that they will build on and then use extensively in fourth grade. Up to second grade, students learn about 17–18 topics. The research clearly confirms that place value is very important (National Council of Teachers of Mathematics, 2000; Sherman, Richardson, & Yard, 2013). Researchers have found that a strong understanding of place value has a positive impact on later mathematics achievement (Miura, Okamato, Chungsoon, & Steere, 1993; Moeller, Pixner, Zuber, Kaufmann, & Nuerk, 2011).

In these lessons we explore how to build an understanding of place value along the learning trajectory so that students understand what it looks like, feels like and how to use it to understand and work with numbers. Students should have plenty of opportunities to practice the big ideas concretely, pictorially and abstractly. Students should have plenty of opportunities to use various tools to explore the concepts. The concepts are the foundation of our math system. Too often, students are rushed through a place value chapter and then the concepts are never addressed again. Place value should be interwoven throughout the year and it should stay up as a workstation center. The National Council of Teachers of Mathematics (NCTM, 2000) notes that students should "use multiple models to develop initial understandings of place value and the base-ten number system."

I want to emphasize that not only should place value blocks be used but also rekenreks, beaded number lines, base ten paper and sketches. Cuisenaire rods and digiblocks are also great tools to use. The idea is that the more ways that students can think about and explore the concept, the more opportunities they have to own it and make sense of it in different ways. The research says that the more ways that students can model concepts the better their understanding. The sample guided math lessons in this chapter take the student through the cycle of concrete, pictorial and abstract to teach:

♦ Adding multi-digit numbers (see Figures 7.1 to 7.71)
♦ Subtracting multi-digit numbers
♦ Rounding to 10 and 100
♦ Multiplying multiples of 10

DOI: 10.4324/9781003169543-7

Research Note 🔍

- A good foundation in place value is essential (National Council of Teachers of Mathematics, 2000; National Research Council, 2009).
- Research consistently finds that students struggle with place and have difficulty understanding tens and ones (Hanich, Jordan, Kaplan, & Dick, 2001; Jordan & Hanich, 2000; Kamii, 1985; Kamii & Joseph, 1988).
- The National Council of Teachers of Mathematics (NCTM, 2000, in their Number and Operations Standards for Grades Pre-K-2) advises for students to "use multiple models to develop initial understandings of place value and the base-ten number system."

Adding Multi-Digit Numbers

Overview

Figure 7.1 Adding Multi-Digit Numbers

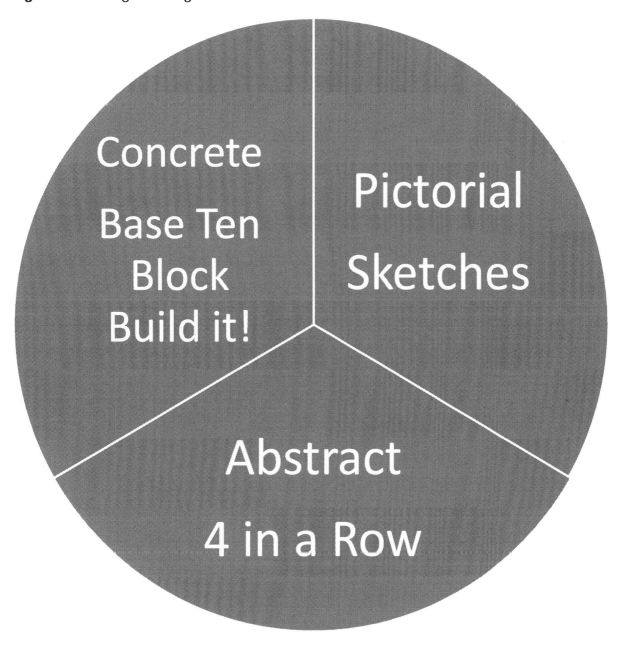

Figure 7.2 Planning Template

Adding Multi-Digit Numbers

Big Idea: We can decompose numbers into hundreds, tens and ones. **Enduring Understanding**: Students will understand that we can add multi-digit numbers using different strategies **Essential Question**: How can we use different strategies to add multi-digit numbers? **I can statement**: I can add multi-digit numbers using different strategies.	**Materials** • Tools: Place Value Blocks • Templates: Ten Frame • Cards • Crayons

Cycle of Engagement

Concrete:

$$200 + 300 = 500$$
$$20 + 30 = 50$$
$$1$$

$$500 + 50 + 1 = 551$$

Pictorial:

Vocabulary & Language Frames

Vocabulary: add, sum, addend, plus, equals, makes, tens, ones, hundreds

Math Talk: I used _____ strategy.

Abstract: 200 Hundred Grid   116 + 32 = 148

1	2	3	4	5	6	7	8	9	10
11	12	13	14	15	16	17	18	19	20
21	22	23	24	25	26	27	28	29	30
31	32	33	34	35	36	37	38	39	40
41	42	43	44	45	46	47	48	49	50
51	52	53	54	55	56	57	58	59	60
61	62	63	64	65	66	67	68	69	70
71	72	73	74	75	76	77	78	79	80
81	82	83	84	85	86	87	88	89	90
91	92	93	94	95	96	97	98	99	100
101	102	103	104	105	106	107	108	109	110
111	112	113	114	115	116	117	118	119	120
121	122	123	124	125	126	127	128	129	130
131	132	133	134	135	136	137	138	139	140
141	142	143	144	145	146	147	148	149	150
151	152	153	154	155	156	157	158	159	160
161	162	163	164	165	166	167	168	169	170
171	172	173	174	175	176	177	178	179	180
181	182	183	184	185	186	187	188	189	190
191	192	193	194	195	196	197	198	199	200

Figure 7.3 Differentiation

Three Differentiated Lessons In this series of lessons, students are working on using different strategies to add multi-digit numbers. They are developing this concept through concrete activities, pictorial activities and abstract activities. Here are some things to think about as you do these lessons.		

Emerging	On Grade Level	Above Grade Level
Do a lot of work with students exploring the strategies with base ten blocks. Make sure that the students have a thorough understanding of all the first and second grade standards.	Be sure to do math sketches along with the representation of the numbers. Students should solve problems and make connections between the model, the sketch and the strategies they are using.	Work with larger numbers.

 Looking for Misunderstandings and Common Errors

Students have trouble with the language of place value. Be sure to do activities and energizers where you unpack the language. For example, students will write two hundred five like this: 2005. So, it is important to work with the actual place and value of numbers. Give problems verbally and have the students write them and then solve them. Also give the students problems both vertically and horizontally.

Figure 7.4 Anchor Chart

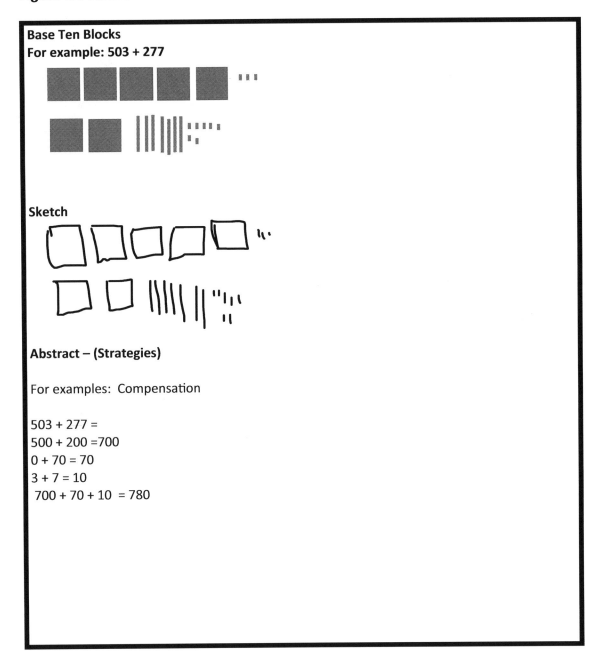

Base Ten Blocks
For example: 503 + 277

Sketch

Abstract – (Strategies)

For examples: Compensation

503 + 277 =
500 + 200 =700
0 + 70 = 70
3 + 7 = 10
 700 + 70 + 10 = 780

Concrete Lesson

Figure 7.5 Concrete Introduction

Introduction to Concrete Explorations	

Launch	**Teacher:** Today we are working on adding multi-digit numbers.
	Vocabulary: Tens, Ones, Hundreds, Expand, Decompose, Sum
	Math Talk:
	My strategy is to _____.
	
	Teacher: Today we are going to work on using different strategies adding 3- digit numbers by breaking them apart, or decomposing them into hundreds, tens and ones. Breaking apart/decomposing is a strategy that we had been working on in the mini-lesson. Here is an example problem: 359 + 267
	Claire: We can add 300 and 200 and that makes 500.
	       Then, 50 + 60 is 110.
	       Then 9 + 7 is 16.
	
	John: So 610 + 16 is 626.
	Teacher: Yep. So why would we want to do it that way?
	Lucy: Because breaking it apart can make it easier.
	Teacher: Who has another way?
	John: I spy a 9. So we could "give and take." So 360 + 266
	Lucy: Even if I did that I would still break it apart. I'd do 500 + 120 + 6.
	Teacher: Ok. I want you guys to use the iPads to model what you did with the virtual manipulatives.
	
	Lucy: You can see 500 + 120 + 6

(Continued)

(Continued)

Model	**Teacher:** So, we have looked at 2 strategies. What is important about strategies? **Ted:** You use them to solve problems. It depends on the numbers. **Teacher:** Let's do another one and talk more about that. What about 147 + 238? **Ted:** Well, I spy an 8 so we can make that a 10…so the problem would then be 145 + 240 and that's easy. **Lucy:** It's 385. **Teacher:** So somebody tell me what he did. **Claire:** He used the 8 to make an easier number. If you see 7, 8 or 9 you could make it into a ten and that probably makes it an easier problem.
Checking for Understanding	**Teacher:** Ok, so I am going to give each one of you a problem to solve. I want you to solve it any way you want and then explain it back to the group. Model it with your virtual manipulatives.

Figure 7.6 Student Activity

	Concrete Student Activity
Guided Practice/ Checking for Understanding	The teacher passes out the problems. Students go around and share their work. **Lucy:** I had 299 + 204. So that's easy because it's 300 + 203 which is 503. You can see I add 1 to 299 and then got 300 + 203. 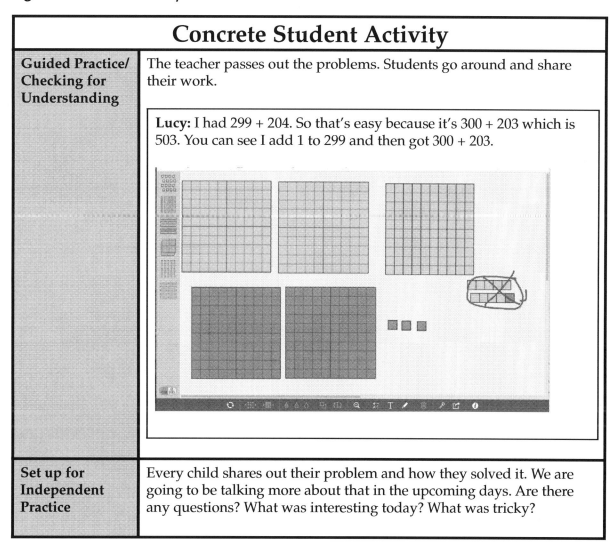
Set up for Independent Practice	Every child shares out their problem and how they solved it. We are going to be talking more about that in the upcoming days. Are there any questions? What was interesting today? What was tricky?

Figure 7.7 Lesson Close

Close
• What did we do today? • What was the math we were practicing? • How did we model the math? • Was this easy or tricky? • Turn to a partner and state one thing you learned today.

Figure 7.8 Addition Cards

422 + 29	333 + 459	531 + 49 +7
780 + 199	876 + 24	776 + 24
905 + 49	189 + 237	288 + 237
222 + 445	275 + 575	343 + 575
127 + 433	382 + 200	497 + 214

Visual Lesson

Figure 7.9 Visual Introduction

<table>
<tr>
<td colspan="2" align="center"><h2>Introduction to Visual Explorations</h2></td>
</tr>
<tr>
<td>Launch</td>
<td>Teacher: Today we are working on building numbers by expanding them out to their place values.
Vocabulary: Tens, Ones, Hundreds, Expand, Decompose, Sum
Math Talk:
• My strategy is to _____.
• I can decompose the numbers by their place and value.
• I can model my strategy with a drawing/math sketch.</td>
</tr>
<tr>
<td>Model</td>
<td>Teacher: Today we are going to continue adding 3-digit numbers. We are going to do it with sketches. We have been doing this in whole group. So let's get started. Here is the first problem. 129 + 88.

Sara: I sketched 129. I made 129 into 130 and then added 130 plus 87

Teacher: Who can explain what she did?

Clark: She made the 129 into 130 on the sketch. 130 plus 80 + 7 is 210 + 7 which is 217.
Tami: I would just add 100 + 110 + 7 and it's still 217.</td>
</tr>
<tr>
<td>Checking for Understanding</td>
<td>Teacher: I am going to give each one of you an equation. I want you to practice representing it with your sketches and write the number in expanded form. Then, you will explain what you did and what the equation is. Who wants to go first?</td>
</tr>
</table>

Figure 7.10 Student Activity

	Visual Student Activity
Guided Practice/ Checking for Understanding	The teacher passes out cards with equations. Students pull a card and represent their thinking. The students each get a chance to share their problem and explain how they solved it. **Teacher:** Sketch out the answer. **Marta:** I sketched 151 + 256. That was easy because I just add 100 and 200 which is 300. Then 50 and 50 is 100. Then 7. So 407. $100 + 50 + 1$ **Teacher:** Who agrees with Marta? Is she correct, if so explain why. **Dan:** I agree with Marta because you can see it in the drawing ...300 plus 100 plus 7. It's 407.
Set up for Independent Practice	*Teacher gives everybody a chance to do and discuss a problem. After everyone has shared the lesson ends.* We are going to be talking more about that in the upcoming days. Are there any questions? What was interesting today? What was tricky?

Figure 7.11 Lesson Close

Close
• What did we do today? • What was the math we were practicing? • How did we model the math? • Was this easy or tricky? • Turn to a partner and state one thing you learned today.

Figure 7.12 Sketch Cards

289 + 200	475 + 199	**202 + 88**
188 + 305	575 + 199	**102 + 144 + 9**
379 + 19	275 + 398	**232 + 109 + 11**
459 + 108	375 + 179	**333 + 55 + 8**
599 + 377	475 + 277	**102 + 109**
609+ 55	575 + 199	**282 + 55**
777 + 9 + 23	37 + 199 + 8	**199 + 9 + 28**

Abstract Lesson

Figure 7.13 Abstract Introduction

	Introduction to Abstract Explorations
Launch	**Teacher:** Today we are going to continue working on multi-digit addition. **Vocabulary:** tens, ones, hundreds, expand, decompose, sum **Math Talk:** My strategy is to _____. I can decompose the numbers by their place and value. I reason about numbers using place and value.
Model	**Teacher:** Today we are going to continue working on addition with multi-digit numbers and focusing on decomposing strategies. Today it is going to be like a riddle. I want you to tell me a problem where the answer is between 230 and 250. **Kelly:** I know. 100 + 134. That's 234. **John:** I know. 150 + 150. No no no . . . that's too high. Wait. 150 + 99? **Teacher:** Are you sure? **John:** I think so because if 150 + 100 is 250 then 99 is 249? I think. **Teacher:** What tool could you use to help you? **John:** The 300 grid. Let me see. (He looks at it. Yep. That's it . . . That works.)
Checking for Understanding	**Teacher:** Ok, today that's what we are going to work on. So put your thinking caps on because I am going to ask you all questions and I want you to come up with some answers.

Figure 7.14 Student Activity

	Abstract Student Activity
Guided Practice/ Checking for Understanding	**Teacher:** Ok. I want you all to think of a problem that has a sum between 152 and 180. **Kelly:** I know. 150 and 27. That makes 177. **John:** I know 100 + 70. **Grace:** I know. 50 + 50 + 79.
Set up for Independent Practice	Teacher calls out various sum ranges. The students come up with the answers and explain what they did. The teacher explains that this game will be one of the choices in the workstations.

Figure 7.15 Lesson Close

Close
• What did we do today? • What was the math we were practicing? • How did we model the math? • Was this easy or tricky? • Turn to a partner and state one thing you learned today.

Figure 7.16 Sum Cards

Sum should be between 150 and 200.	Sum should be between 390 and 401.	Sum should be between 302 and 310.
Sum should be between 250 and 300.	Sum should be between 190 and 201.	Sum should be between 405 and 459.
Sum should be between 150 and 200.	Sum should be between 390 and 401.	Sum should be between 500 and 510.
Sum should be between 250 and 300.	Sum should be between 101 and 135.	Sum should be between 777 and 790.
Sum should be between 750 and 795.	Sum should be between 602 and 607.	Sum should be between 808 and 830.

Section Summary

When working with multi-digit numbers, it is important to have students build them draw them and solve them using mental math. It is also really important to have students solve them in many different ways. You want to build flexibility around number. The point is to provide many opportunities for students to work with hundreds, tens and ones throughout the year, not only during the place value unit of study.

Subtracting 3-Digit Numbers

Overview

Figure 7.17 Overview

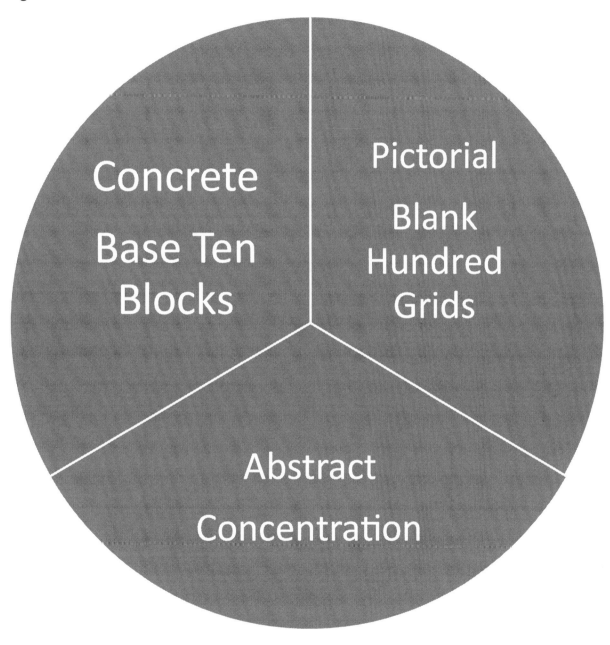

Figure 7.18 Planning Template

Introduction to Concrete Explorations: Subtracting 3-digit Numbers

Big Idea: Using place value you can model subtraction of multi-digit numbers. **Enduring Understanding:** We can model problems in many ways. **Essential Question:** What are the ways to model this type of problem? **I can statement:** I can model subtracting 3-digit numbers in many ways.	**Materials** • Tools: Base ten blocks • Templates: Ten Frame • Cards • Crayons

Cycle of Engagement **Concrete: 232 - 110** 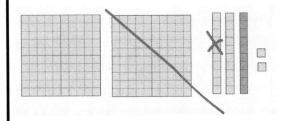 **Pictorial: Drawing. (220 – 210)**  Abstract $281 - 199 = 282 - 200 = 82$	**Vocabulary & Language Frames** • Count Up • Count Back • Compensate

Figure 7.19 Differentiated Lessons

Three Differentiated Lessons

In this series of lessons, students are working on the concept of subtracting 3-digit numbers. They are developing this concept through concrete activities, pictorial activities and abstract activities. Here are some things to think about as you do these lessons.

Emerging	On Grade Level	Above Grade Level
Do a lot of work with students subtracting 3-digit numbers with place value blocks. Review subtracting 2-digit numbers first.	The grade level standard is that students can subtract 3- and 4-digit numbers. Work through the cycle of concrete, pictorial and abstract representations.	Work with larger numbers.

 Looking for Misunderstandings and Common Errors

Students have a great deal of trouble with subtraction. Do a lot of work with base ten blocks and sketches. The focus should be on building strategic competence rather than just rushing to traditional algorithms.

Figure 7.20 Anchor Chart

Subtracting 3-digit numbers

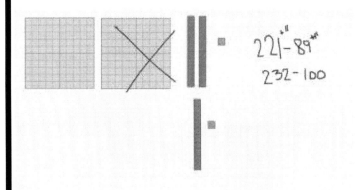

$$221 - 89$$
$$232 - 100$$

Sketch: 262 – 199 = 263 - 200

Concrete Lesson

Figure 7.21 Concrete Introduction

<table>
<tr>
<td colspan="2" align="center"><h2>Introduction to Concrete/Visual Explorations</h2></td>
</tr>
<tr>
<td>Launch</td>
<td>

Teacher: Today we are going to work on subtracting 3-digit numbers.

Vocabulary: add, ten, sum, addend, plus, equals, makes

Math Talk: My strategy is _____. My model is _____.

</td>
</tr>
<tr>
<td>Model</td>
<td>

Teacher: Today we are going to continue to work on subtracting multi-digit problems. You can use whatever strategy makes since for you. $400 - 285$. I want to show you how to use the strategy of counting up. I am going to show you a couple of ways. First we are going to do it with the place value blocks. Notice that I can start with 285 and count up to 400. Watch.

Next we are going to do it using hundred grids. We will use these to visualize our thinking and eventually you will have a mental map for this.

Teacher- "I notice that we are working with a number that has zeros (400). When I am subtracting across zeroes, it can be helpful to count up. I can use the 500 grid to help me visualize the counting up. So if I start with 285 and I want to count up to 400, it will help me to get the 285 as close to a multiple of 100. The next multiple of 100 that I see on my 500 grid, is 300 and to get to 300, I would need to add 15. Once I am at 300, I can add 100 more to get to 400. So the difference between 400 and 285 is the sum of my jumps 15+100, which is 115."

</td>
</tr>
</table>

(Continued)

(Continued)

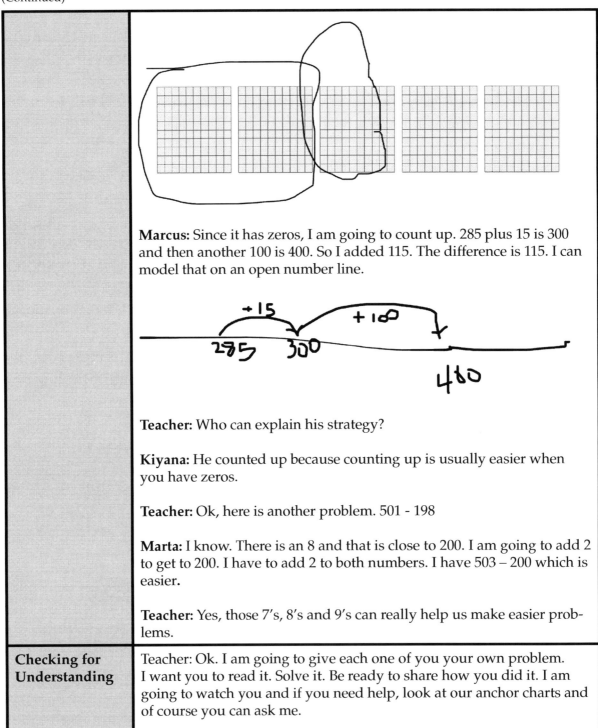

Marcus: Since it has zeros, I am going to count up. 285 plus 15 is 300 and then another 100 is 400. So I added 115. The difference is 115. I can model that on an open number line.

Teacher: Who can explain his strategy?

Kiyana: He counted up because counting up is usually easier when you have zeros.

Teacher: Ok, here is another problem. 501 - 198

Marta: I know. There is an 8 and that is close to 200. I am going to add 2 to get to 200. I have to add 2 to both numbers. I have 503 – 200 which is easier.

Teacher: Yes, those 7's, 8's and 9's can really help us make easier problems.

| Checking for Understanding | Teacher: Ok. I am going to give each one of you your own problem. I want you to read it. Solve it. Be ready to share how you did it. I am going to watch you and if you need help, look at our anchor charts and of course you can ask me. |

Figure 7.22 Concrete Student Activity

	Concrete Student Activity
Guided Practice/ Checking for Understanding	The teacher passes out the problems. Students pull a card and explain their thinking. The students each get a chance to share their problem and explain how they solved it.
	Ted: My problem is 1000 – 899. That's easy I can count up. Add 1 to 899 to make 900 and then another 100. The difference is 101.
	Timmy: My problem was 500 – 250. I had 250 and I counted up 250 more to get 500.
	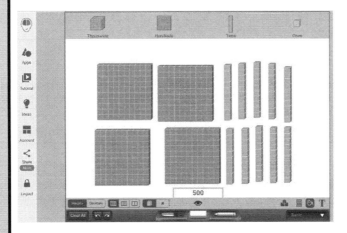
	Kelly: I got 727 – 589. I just counted up. I added 11 to get to 600. Then I added 127. 127 plus 11 is 138. The difference is 138. So at first it looked hard but if you get to 100 it's easy.
	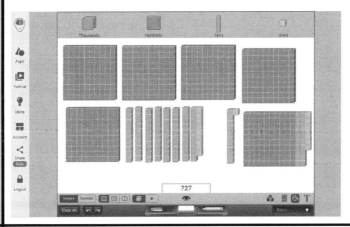
Set up for Independent Practice	Every child shares out there problem and how they solved it there problem. Teacher: We are going to be talking more about that in the upcoming days. Are there any questions? What was interesting today? What was tricky?

Figure 7.23 Lesson Close

Close
• What did we do today? • What was the math we were practicing? • How did we model the math? • Was this easy or tricky? • Turn to a partner and state one thing you learned today.

Figure 7.24 Cards

180 101	207 - 108
235 - 104	432 - 205
520 - 352	1000 - 788
650 - 499	1000 - 999
975 - 589	Make up your own problem!

Figure 7.25 Challenge version

310 - __ = 105	1000 - __ = 131
__ - 100 = 700	__ - 109 = 150
__ - 305 = 500	479 - __ = 145
__ - 199 = 305	__ - 285 = 192
__ -210 = 405	__ - 199 = 300

Visual Lesson

Figure 7.26 Visual Introduction

<table>
<tr>
<td colspan="2"><h2>Introduction to More Visual explorations</h2></td>
</tr>
<tr>
<td>Launch</td>
<td>

Teacher: Today we are going to continue working on subtracting 3- digit numbers. We will continue looking at how we can do that pictorially.

Vocabulary: count up, ten, hundred, plus, equals, makes, subtract,

Math Talk:
- My model was _____.
- My Strategy was _____.

</td>
</tr>
<tr>
<td>Model</td>
<td>

Teacher: Today I want to focus on modeling on the number line. 325 − 298.
Who wants to try it? How could you use a number line to find the difference between 325 and 298?
Katie: I can start at 298 and jump to 300 and then jump 25. I jumped 27 In total.

Teacher: Who can name the strategy that she used?

Kelly: She counted up.

Teacher: What about 400 − 357?
Hong: I can do it. So, it's zeros. I go from 357 to 360. (so that's plus 3 and then 40 more to get to 400. That is 43).

Teacher: What is 43?

Kayla: The difference.

</td>
</tr>
<tr>
<td>Checking for Understanding</td>
<td>

Teacher: I am going to give each one of you an equation. I want you to practice representing it with your hundred grid mat. Then, you will explain what you did and what the equation is. Who wants to go first?

</td>
</tr>
</table>

Figure 7.27 Student Activity

	Visual Student Activity
Guided Practice/ Checking for Understanding	The teacher passes out cards with equations. Students pull a card and represent their thinking. The students each get a chance to share their problem and explain how they solved it. **Grace:** I got 500 – 299. That's so easy. Plus 1 to 300 and then 200 makes it 201. 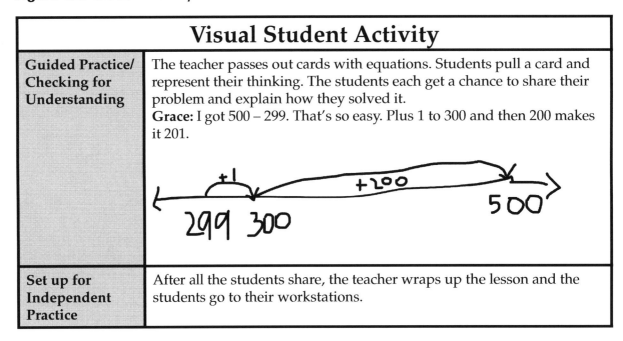
Set up for Independent Practice	After all the students share, the teacher wraps up the lesson and the students go to their workstations.

Figure 7.28 Lesson Close

Close
• What did we do today? • What was the math we were practicing? • How did we model the math? • Was this easy or tricky? • Turn to a partner and state one thing you learned today.

Figure 7.29 Open Number Lines

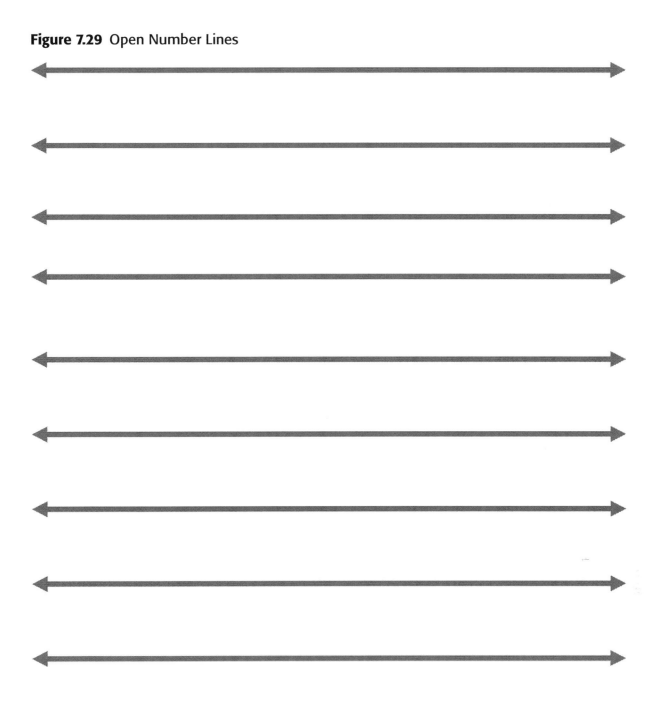

Abstract Lesson

Figure 7.30 Abstract Introduction

Introduction to Abstract Explorations

Launch	**Teacher:** Today we are going to work on subtracting with different strategies. **Vocabulary: minuend, subtrahend, subtraction, take away, model, strategy, place value, break apart, compensation, move the number line** **Math Talk:** My strategy is _____. My model is _____.
Model	**Teacher:** Today we are going to continue to work on subtracting multi-digit problems. We will be working with missing numbers. You can use whatever strategy makes sense for you. **Here is the problem: ____ − 50 = 250.** How might we go about figuring this one out? **Marcus:** We did this on the rug. I know. We add 50 and 250. That give us 300 and 300 − 50 is 250. You have to add the 2 numbers! **Teacher:** Who can explain his strategy? **Kiyana:** He added the answer and the part we took away to get the big number. **Teacher:** Ok, here is another problem. ____ − 46 = 100. **Marta:** I know. 146 − 46 is 100. **Tami:** It's kinda easy. You just have to add those 2 numbers. **Teacher:** But why does that work? **Kelli:** Because you are looking for the larger number. So you add the 2 parts together.
Checking for Understanding	**Teacher:** Ok. I am going to give each one of you your own problem. I want you to read it. Solve it. Be ready to share how you did it. I am going to watch you and if you need help, look at our anchor charts and of course you can ask me.

Figure 7.31 Student Activity

	Abstract Student Activity
Guided Practice/ Checking for Understanding	The teacher passes out the problems. Students pull a card and act out their problems. The students each get a chance to share their problem and explain how they solved it.

Ted: My problem is ____ - 189 = 250.

Timmy: This is tricky.

Teacher: Ok, why?

Timmy: The numbers are harder.

Kelly: We can add 100 to make 350. And then 50 to make 400. Then 39. So, that's 439.

Teacher: What's 439?

Todd: The missing number.

Marta: So 439 minus 189 is 250.

Teacher: Did everybody follow her? Kelly can you do that on paper?

Kelly: |
| **Set up for Independent Practice** | Every child shares out their problem and how they solved it there problem.
Teacher: We are going to be talking more about that in the upcoming days. Are there any questions? What was interesting today? What was tricky? |

Figure 7.32 Close

Close
• What did we do today?
• What was the math we were practicing?
• How did we model the math?
• Was this easy or tricky?
• Turn to a partner and state one thing you learned today.

Figure 7.33 Subtraction Cards

___ -101 = 205	___ - 108 = 200
___ - 104 = 541	___ - 205 = 500
___ - 352 = 50	___ - 788 - 50
___ - 499 = 101	___ - 999 = 2
___ - 589 = 101	Make up your own problem!

Figure 7.34 Challenge Version

310 - ___ = 105	1000 - ___ = 131
___ - 100 = 700	___ - 109 = 150
___ - 305 = 500	479 - ___ = 145
___ - 199 = 305	___ - 285 = 192
___ -210 = 405	___ - 199 = 300

Section Summary

Subtracting 3-digits numbers can be tricky for students. It is important to spend time working on concrete, pictorial and abstract examples. The work is around getting students to be comfortable with different types of numbers. Students will look at a problem and decide that it is hard just because of the way that it looks. It is important to get them to stop and think about the numbers and their relationship to each other and then what strategies they could use to deal with those numbers. So, they should just think about counting up when they see subtraction across zeros, in many if not most cases. It is just easier. They should look for sevens, eights and nines so that they can get to the nearest ten or hundred. Subtraction should be worked on throughout the year, certainly not just during the current unit of study. It should be integrated throughout routines and energizers as well as to put it in the year-long place value workstation.

Rounding to the Nearest Ten

Overview

Figure 7.35 Overview

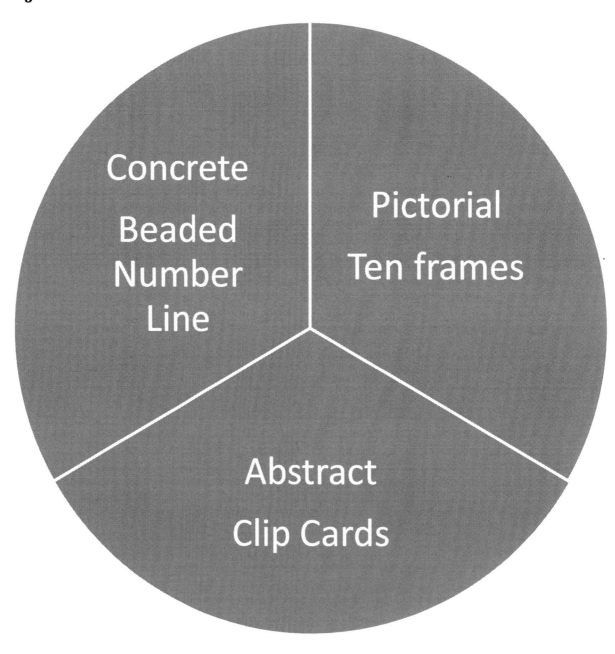

Figure 7.36 Rounding 2-Digit Numbers

Rounding Numbers

Big Idea: Using Place Value you can round numbers to the nearest 10 **Enduring Understanding:** We can model problems in many ways. **Essential Question:** What are the ways to model rounding? **I can statement:** I can round numbers to the nearest 10 in different ways.	**Materials** • Tools: Rekenrek • Tools: Beaded Number Line • Templates: Ten Frames • Cards • Crayons
Cycle of Engagement **Concrete:** Abstract: 54 54 rounds to 50	Vocabulary & Language Frames **Tens, rounding, round, nearest ten** **I can round ____ to _____.** **Pictorial: Drawing**

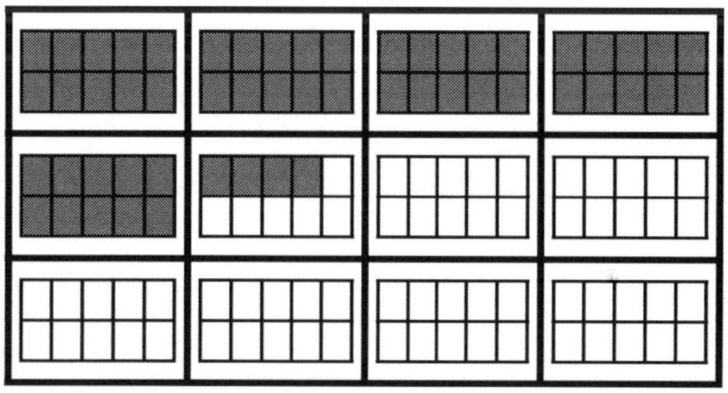

Figure 7.37 Differentiation

Three Differentiated Lessons		
In this series of lessons, students are working on the concept of rounding to 10. They are developing this concept through concrete activities, pictorial activities and abstract activities. Here are some things to think about as you do these lessons.		
Emerging	**On Grade Level**	**Above Grade Level**
Do a lot of work with models. Use the beaded number line and the base ten blocks.	It is really important to ask students open questions where they have to come up with the numbers that would round to a certain number. For example ask them, "Give me 3 numbers that round to 70."	Extend the number range. Have students make up their own problems.

 Looking for Misunderstandings and Common Errors

Too often we rely on poems and songs to teach rounding. Be sure to have the students talk about the number line and the relationship of the numbers.

Figure 7.38 Anchor Chart

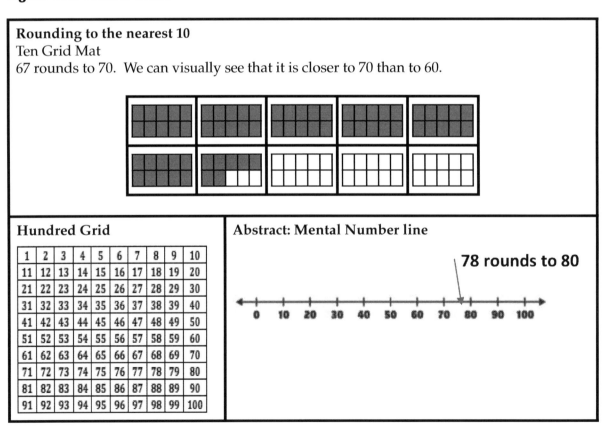

Rounding to the nearest 10
Ten Grid Mat
67 rounds to 70. We can visually see that it is closer to 70 than to 60.

Hundred Grid

Abstract: Mental Number line

78 rounds to 80

Concrete Lesson

Figure 7.39 Concrete Introduction

Introduction to Concrete Explorations

Launch	**Teacher:** Today we are going to work on rounding 2-digit numbers using our beaded number line. **Vocabulary:** tens, nearest ten, rounds, rounding **Math Talk:** It is in between ____ and ____. ____ rounds to _____.
Model	**Teacher:** Hi. So here is the beaded number line. I want to know how you can round 87 to the nearest ten. **Jason:** I can. See you can find 87. It is between 80 and 90. It rounds to 90. **Teacher:** That's a great way. Who agrees? **Cynthia:** I do because it is closer to 90 than 80.
Checking for Understanding	*Teacher reads 2 more problems that the group discusses.* **Teacher:** Ok. I am going to give each one of you your own problem. I want you to read it. Solve it. Be ready to share how you did it. I am going to watch you and if you need help, look at our anchor charts and of course you can ask me.

Figure 7.40 Concrete Student Activity

	Concrete Student Activities
Guided Practice/ Checking for Understanding	The teacher passes out the problems. Each student has their own beaded number line. Students pull a card and act out their problems. The students each get a chance to share their problem and explain how they solved it. **Timmy:** My problem is 42: 42 is in between ___ and ___. I rounds to ____. **Timmy:** 42 is in between 40 and 50. It rounds to 40. **Teacher:** Great. Who agrees with him and why? **Kelly:** Well, it is really close to 40. So it rounds to 40. 
Set up for Independent Practice	Every child shares out their problem and how they solved it on the beaded number line. We are going to be talking more about that in the upcoming days. Are there any questions? What was interesting today? What was tricky?

Figure 7.41 Lesson Close

Close
• What did we do today?   • What was the math we were practicing?   • How did we model the math?   • Was this easy or tricky?   • Turn to a partner and state one thing you learned today.

Figure 7.42 Rounding 2-Digit Numbers

81 81 is in between ___ and ___. It rounds to ___.	**44** 44 is in between ___ and ___. It rounds to ___.
32 81 is in between ___ and ___. It rounds to ___.	**26** 26 is in between ___ and ___. It rounds to ___.
55 55 is in between ___ and ___. It rounds to ___.	**89** 89 is in between ___ and ___. It rounds to ___.
68 68 is in between ___ and ___. It rounds to ___.	**77** 77 is in between ___ and ___. It rounds to ___.
11 11 is in between ___ and ___. It rounds to ___.	**Make up your own problem!**

Figure 7.43 Challenge Version

Give us 2 numbers that round to 10.	Give us 2 numbers that round to 20.
Give us 2 numbers that round to 30.	Give us 2 numbers that round to 40.
Give us 2 numbers that round to 50.	Give us 2 numbers that round to 60.
Give us 2 numbers that round to 70.	Give us 2 numbers that round to 80.
Give us 2 numbers that round to 90.	Give us 2 numbers that round to 100.
Give us 2 numbers that round to 110.	Give us 2 numbers that round to 120.
Give us 2 numbers that round to 130.	Give us 2 numbers that round to 150.

Visual Lesson

Figure 7.44 Visual Introduction

<table>
<tr>
<td colspan="2"><h2 align="center">Introduction to Visual Explorations</h2> I am learning to add two 2-digit numbers. </td>
</tr>
<tr>
<td>Launch</td>
<td>

Teacher: Today we are going to work on rounding 2-digit numbers .

Vocabulary: tens, nearest ten, rounds, rounding

Math Talk: It is in between ____ and _____. ____ rounds to _____.

</td>
</tr>
<tr>
<td>Model</td>
<td>

Teacher: Today we are going to continue working on rounding. We will be looking at how we can do that pictorially with our ten-frame mat.

Teacher: Notice what I have here. This is our ten frame hundred mat that we have worked with before. Today we are going to do shading to round numbers. So for example, I have a picture here. Who can tell me what number is represented and what is the nearest ten.

</td>
</tr>
<tr>
<td>Checking for Understanding</td>
<td>

Kelly: I see 68. It rounds to 70. You can see it is close to 70. There is only 2 more to get to 70.

</td>
</tr>
</table>

Figure 7.45 Student Activity

	Visual Student Activity
Guided Practice/ Checking for Understanding	The teacher passes out cards with equations. Students pull a card and solve it. The students each get a chance to share their problem and explain how they solved it. **Marta:** I got [73] So, I can see that it rounds to 70. It is closer to 70 than 80. 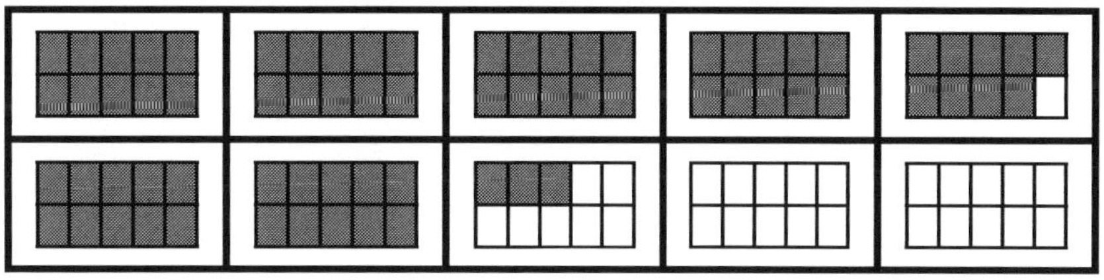
Set up for Independent Practice	*Teacher gives everybody a chance to do and discuss a problem. After everyone has shared the lesson ends.* ***Teacher:*** *We are going to be talking more about that in the upcoming days. Are there any questions? What was interesting today? What was tricky?*

Figure 7.46 Lesson Close

Close
• What did we do today? • What was the math we were practicing? • How did we model the math? • Was this easy or tricky? • Turn to a partner and state one thing you learned today.

Figure 7.47 Ten Frame Shading Cards

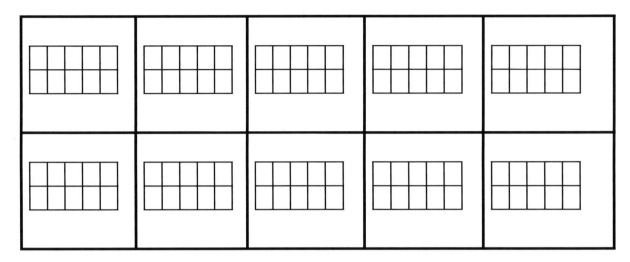

Figure 7.48 Expression Cards

85	44
37	28
55	16
88	63
91	Make up your own problem!

Figure 7.49 Abstract Introduction

	Introduction to Abstract Explorations
Launch	**Teacher:** Today we are going to work on rounding 2-digit numbers . **Vocabulary:** tens, nearest ten, rounds, rounding **Math Talk:** It is in between ____ and _____. ____ rounds to _____.
Model	**Teacher:** Today we are going to play Round It. Players each get 7 cards. Place the cards face up in front of them. The rest of the deck is split between the two players. They each turn over a card at the same time. They try to match one of their cards to that card. They are rounding their cards to the nearest ten. If you can't match the card then you just have to wait until you all pull again and try to match that card. The first person to cover all 7 of their cards wins. You can use any of our tools or templates to help you if you get stuck. I am going to play against you two teams. Teacher: 20 51 23 28 35 78 86 94 So I have a match because 23 rounds to 20. So I'll cover that number.

(Continued)

	Team 1: [60] [81] [29] [38] [45] [88] [96] [72] So, we don't have a match yet. Nothing we have rounds to 60. Team 2: [50] [62] [33] [89] [55] [21] [92] [44]
Checking for Understanding	We don't have a match either! Nothing we have rounds to 50. What would be a number that would be a match with 50? Timmy: 52 Ok, let's keep playing.

Abstract Lesson

Figure 7.50 Student Activity

	Abstract Student Activity
Guided Practice/ Checking for Understanding	The teacher continues to play the game with the students. They spend the entire time playing this game. They discuss rounding and how to think about it. The teacher is also noticing what the students are doing and how they are using tools to check their thinking if they need to. . <table><tr><td>Terri She can do it</td><td>Katie She looks at the number line sometimes.</td></tr><tr><td>Chung He gets it but sometimes questions himself</td><td>Lisa She uses the hundred grid often</td></tr></table>
Set up for Independent Practice	The students continue to play the game until they are done. The teacher watches how the students are doing, who knows the answer right away and who gets stuck. She also notices who has to use their tools and who just knows it by heart.

Figure 7.51 Lesson Close

Close
• What did we do today?
• What was the math we were practicing?
• How did we model the math?
• Was this easy or tricky?
• Turn to a partner and state one thing you learned today.

Figure 7.52 Number Cards

32	44	56	68	75
88	91	23	15	53
61	99	29	36	47
29	33	17	82	71
77	64	55	41	96
10	20	30	40	50
60	70	80	90	100

Section Summary

Rounding numbers can be tricky. Students need a lot of opportunities to think about the idea of rounding and a good understanding of relationships of numbers on the number line. It is important to start with the beaded number line and then use the marked number line and then also use the ten frame grid and the number grid. Give students plenty of opportunities to play around with rounding and many different games where they can use tools. Have them explain what they are doing as they do it.

Multiplying Multiples of 10 by a Single Digit

Overview

Figure 7.53 Overview

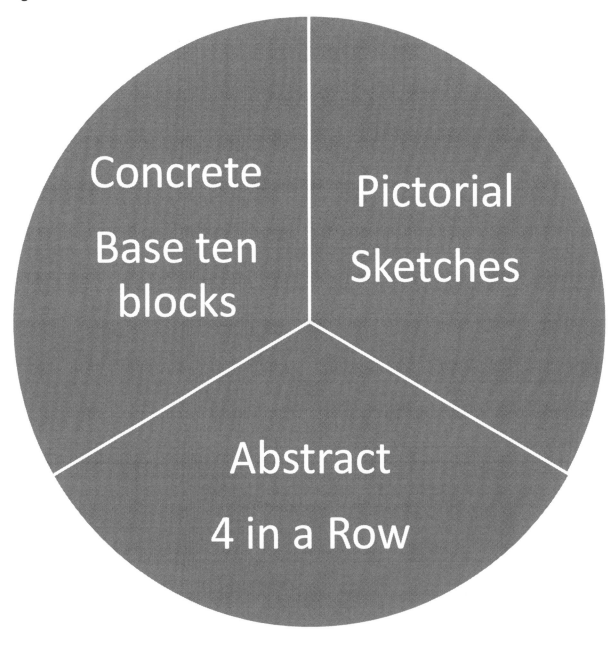

Figure 7.54 Planning Template

Multiplying Multiples of Ten

Big Idea: Place Value **Enduring Understanding:** Students will understand that there are patterns when working with numbers. **Essential Question:** What are the ways to model multiplying multiples of ten? **I can statement:** I can multiply multiples of ten and explain my thinking.	**Materials** • Tools: Beaded Number Line • Templates: Ten Frame • Cards • Crayons • Base ten blocks • Hundred grid

Cycle of Engagement

Concrete:

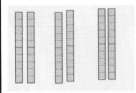

Pictorial: Drawing

Vocabulary & Language Frames

• Tens, Ones, Hundreds
• Compare
• Greater than
• Less than
• Equal to

_____ is greater than_____.
_____ is less than_____.
_____ is the same as _____.

Abstract: Hundred Grid

1	2	3	4	5	6	7	8	9	10
11	12	13	14	15	16	17	18	19	20
21	22	23	24	25	26	27	28	29	30
31	32	33	34	35	36	37	38	39	40
41	42	43	44	45	46	47	48	49	50
51	52	53	54	55	56	57	58	59	60
61	62	63	64	65	66	67	68	69	70
71	72	73	74	75	76	77	78	79	80
81	82	83	84	85	86	87	88	89	90
91	92	93	94	95	96	97	98	99	100

Figure 7.55 Differentiated Lessons

Three Differentiated Lessons		
In this series of lessons, students are working on the concept of multiplying multiples of 10. They are developing this concept through concrete activities, pictorial activities and abstract activities. Here are some things to think about as you do these lessons.		
Emerging	**On Grade Level**	**Above Grade Level**
Do a lot of work with students using base ten blocks. You can begin the journey with 100 beaded rekenrek as well.	Make sure students can sketch their thinking. Also use base ten paper because it is a great visual.	Work with larger numbers.

 Looking for Misunderstandings and Common Errors

The focus here should be that students look at patterns. They should explain what they are seeing and how the pattern works in place value language.

Figure 7.56 Anchor Chart

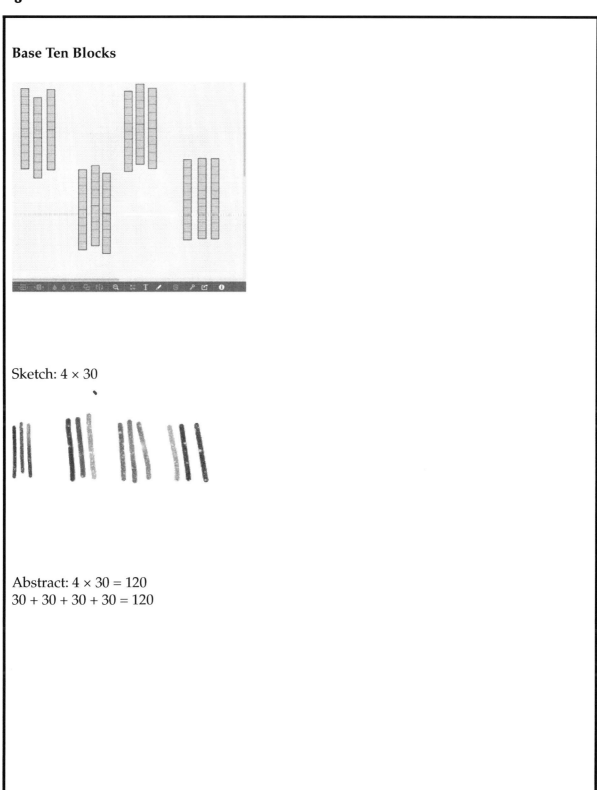

Base Ten Blocks

Sketch: 4×30

Abstract: $4 \times 30 = 120$
$30 + 30 + 30 + 30 = 120$

Concrete Lesson

Figure 7.57 Concrete Introduction

Introduction to Concrete Explorations	
Launch	**Teacher:** Today we are going to work on multiplying multiples of ten by a single digit number.

Vocabulary: multiply, single digit, multiples of ten, strategies

Math Talk: I multiplied ____ by _____. The product is _____. |
| **Model** | **Teacher:** Who could tell me what a multiple of ten is?

Carole: Like if you skip count by that number.

Teacher: Yes, give me an example…

Carole: Like 10, 20, 30, 40

Teacher: So let's look at what happens when you multiply a multiple of ten by a single digit number. Let's do 2×20.

Mike: That's easy it is 40. It's 20 plus 20.
Teacher: Ok, model it and explain the model with the base ten blocks. How can we describe this model? How many groups are there? How many are in each group?

Marisol: There are 2 groups. Each group has 20.

Teacher: Yes, we can represent the equation 2×20 as 2 groups of 20. |

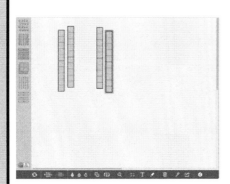

Teacher: Ok, so how could we represent 4 × 20?

Saul: We can make 4 groups and put 20 in each group.

Kiyana: I can solve that by thinking about multiplying 4 × 2 which is 8. So 4 groups of 20 would be 80.

Teacher: So, you used a helper fact. Great thinking. Can we model that?

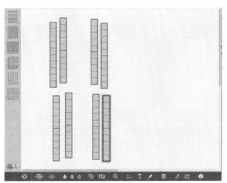

Marta: It looks like this.

Checking for Understanding	**Teacher:** Yes and notice that 2 times 20 was 40 and then if we did 4 it just doubled. Does everybody see that strategy? So far we have talked about 2 different ways of thinking about it. I am going to give each one of you different cards. I want you to model it on your ipads and then discuss it with us and explain what you did. **Teacher:** Any questions? Ok, here are your cards.

Figure 7.58 Student Activity

	Concrete Student Activity
Guided Practice/ Checking for Understanding	The teacher passes out the problems. Students pull a card and act out their problems. The students each get a chance to share their problem and explain how they solved it. **Mia:** I got 5 × 20. I can represent that by making 5 groups of 20. So I know that 5 × 2 is 10 so 5 groups of 20 is equal to 100. It looks like this.
Set up for Independent Practice	Every child shares out their problem and how they solved it. We are going to be talking more about that in the upcoming days. Are there any questions? What was interesting today? What was tricky?

Figure 7.59 Lesson Close

Close
• What did we do today? • What was the math we were practicing? • How did we model the math? • Was this easy or tricky? • Turn to a partner and state one thing you learned today.

Figure 7.60 Cards

5×20	3×40
7×20	8×40
4×30	3×30
5×50	3×50
5×60	3×70
2×80	3×90

Visual Lesson

Figure 7.61 Visual Introduction

Introduction to a Visual Activity
I am learning to compare numbers

Launch	**Teacher:** Today we are going to continue working on multiplying multiples of ten. We are going to do it with a sketch. **Vocabulary:** ones, tens, hundreds, greater than, less than, same as, equal to **Math Talk:** The helper fact is _____. Or My strategy is _____.
Model	**Teacher:** Here is our first problem: 2×30? I want you all to model it on your paper. **Hong:** I drew 2 groups of 30 and it shows 60. But I know that 2×30 is 60 because $30 + 30$ is 60.  ||| |||
Checking for Understanding	**Teacher:** I am going to give each one of you an equation. I want you to practice representing it with your sketches. Then, you will explain what you did and what the equation is. Who wants to go first?

Figure 7.62 Student Activity

	Visual Student Activity
Guided Practice/ Checking for Understanding	The teacher passes out cards with equations. Students pull a card and represent their thinking. The students each get a chance to share their problem and explain how they solved it. **Sean:** I got this problem. 4×50. I know that $50 + 50$ is 100 and then again, it is 100 so that's 200. 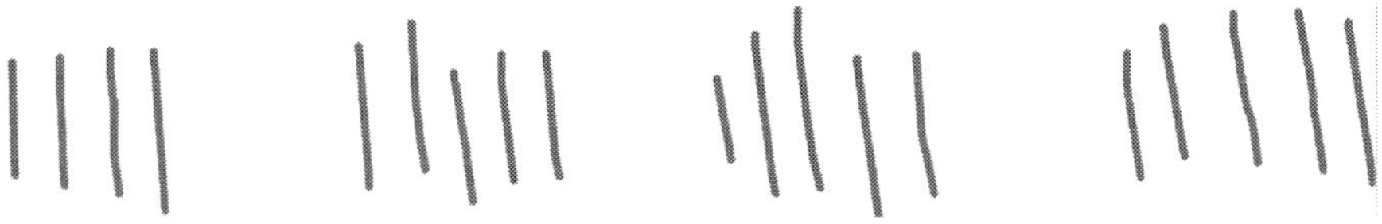 |||| ||||| ||||| || |||
Set up for Independent Practice	*Teacher gives everybody a chance to do and discuss a problem. After everyone has shared the lesson ends.* We are going to be talking more about that in the upcoming days. Are there any questions? What was interesting today? What was tricky?

Figure 7.63 Lesson Close

Close
• What did we do today?   • What was the math we were practicing?   • How did we model the math?   • Was this easy or tricky?   • Turn to a partner and state one thing you learned today.

Figure 7.64 Cards

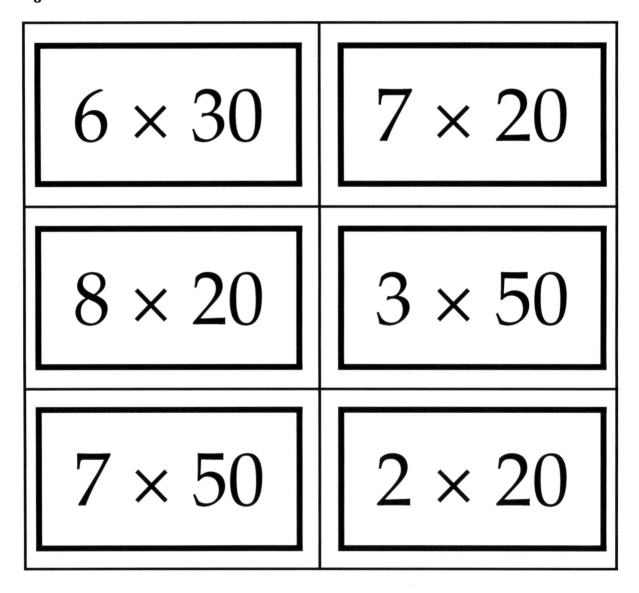

(Continued)

2×30	4×30
8×30	3×40
5×50	9×20

Abstract Lesson

Figure 7.65 Abstract Introduction

	Introduction to Abstract Explorations
Launch	**Teacher:** Today we are going to work on multiplying multiples of 10 by a single digit.
	Vocabulary: multiply, single digit, multiples of 10, strategies
	Math Talk:
	The helper fact is _____.
	My strategy is _____.
Model	**Teacher:** Here are two numbers: 2 × 40. Tell me how we can think about solving this.
	Carole: I know it is 80. Because it is 40 doubled. That's easy.
	Teacher: Yes. Tell me how you knew to double it.
	Carole: Because it was being multiplied by 2.
	Teacher: What if it was being multiplied by 4?
	Mike: We could think 80 doubled, which is 160.
	Teacher: What if it was 8 × 40?
	Mike: We could double 160. That's tricky.
	Teacher: Whose got an idea?
	Marta: I could add the 100's and then the 60. So that's 200 + 120 is 320.
	Teacher: Who agrees?
	Todd: I do. Because 16 plus 16 is 32 so that would be 320.
Checking for Understanding	**Teacher:** Tell me about what we were doing in terms of thinking about the problems?
	Marta: We were using the double, double double and double, double, double strategies.
	Teacher: That's right. We are going to be doing a lot of these problems, but I want you all to think about your strategies and use them for coming up with the answers. So the game we are going to play today is 4 in a row. Everybody knows how to play it, so we are going to do it but this time we are working on multiplying by multiples of 10. Remember the strategies that you can use. When you make a match you have to explain to your partner what your strategy was. I will also be asking you all questions as you play the game.

Figure 7.66 Student Activity

	Abstract Student Activity
Guided Practice/ Checking for Understanding	**Students play the game. They discuss their strategies.** **Teacher:** Melanie, how did you solve 7×90? **Melanie:** I used a helper fact. I used 7×9 and got 63 and then I made it 630. **Teacher:** Juan, what was your strategy for solving 5×50? **Juan:** I know that 5×5 is 25. So then this is 250.
Set up for Independent Practice	The teacher continues to ask the students questions about their strategies as they play the game. The teacher is taking notes as the students play. They are using their different strategies to explain their thinking.

Figure 7.67 Lesson Close

Close
• What did we do today? • What was the math we were practicing? • How did we model the math? • Was this easy or tricky? • Turn to a partner and state one thing you learned today.

Figure 7.68 4 in a Row

4 in a Row Game Monkeying around with numbers: Pull a card and cover the product. Each player uses a different set of color counters. Whoever gets 4 in a row wins.				
180	140	60	120	50
160	150	270	720	300
80	100	350	210	350
200	90	250	640	490
40	360	450	810	280

Figure 7.69 Cards

9×20	7×20	2×30	6×20	5×10
8×20	3×50	9×30	8×90	5×60
8×10	5×20	7×50	7×30	5×70
5×40	9×10	5×50	8×80	7×70
2×20	4×90	9×50	9×90	4×70

Section Summary

When working with the third graders on multiplying multiples of 10 it is important to take them through the cycle of concrete, pictorial and abstract. They have to see it and work with different manipulatives to do it. They should use base ten blocks and the beaded number line. For the visual work, use sketches but also use base ten paper so students can visually see the tens. It is important that students can verbalize their strategies.

Depth of Knowledge

Depth of Knowledge is a framework that encourages us to ask questions that require that students think, reason, explain, defend and justify their thinking (Webb, 2002). Here is snapshot of what that can look like in terms of place value work.

Figure 7.70 DOK Activities

	What are different strategies and models that we can use to teach multi-digit addition with place and value?	What are different strategies and models that we can use to teach multi-digit subtraction with place value?	What are different strategies and models that we can use to teach rounding?	What are different strategies and models that we can use for multiplying a single digit by a multiple of ten?
DOK Level 1 (These are questions where students are required to simply recall/reproduce an answer/do a procedure.)	How many hundreds, tens and ones are in this number? How can we break them apart to add?	Solve 400 – 145	Round 53 to the nearest ten	Multiply 3 × 50
DOK Level 2 (These are questions where students have to use information, think about concepts and reason.) This is considered a more challenging problem than a level 1 problem.	Can you solve 234 + 198 in 2 different ways?	Can you solve 400 – 259 in 2 different ways?	Can you give me 3 numbers that round to 90?	Model and solve 2 × 70 in 2 different ways
DOK Level 3 (These are questions where students have to reason, plan, explain, justify and defend their thinking.)	Can you give me a problem that has a sum between 475 and 500? Tell me 2 ways to solve it.	Can you find and fix the error? 400 – 199 = 399	Tell me a story where I would need to round something to the nearest ten.	What are some problems that have 120 as the product as the result of multiplying a single digit by a multiple of 10? Explain your thinking.

Adapted from Kaplinsky (https://robertkaplinsky.com/depth-knowledge-matrix-elementary-math/). A great resource for asking open questions is Marion Small's *Good Questions: Great ways to differentiate mathematics instruction in the standards-based classroom* (2017).

Also, Robert Kaplinsky has done a great job in pushing our thinking forward with the Depth of Knowledge Matrices he created. The Kentucky Department of Education (2007) also has great DOK Math Matrices.

Figure 7.71 Asking Rigorous Questions

DOK 1	DOK 2 **At this level students explain their thinking.**	DOK 3 **At this level students have to justify, defend and prove their thinking with objects, drawings and diagrams.**
What is the answer to ??? Can you model the number? Can you model the problem? Can you identify the answer that matches this equation? How many hundreds, tens and ones are in this number?	How do you know that the equation is correct? Can you pick the correct answer and explain why it is correct? How can you model that problem? What is another way to model that problem? Can you model that on the . . . ??? Give me an example of a . . . type of problem. Which answer is incorrect? Explain your thinking	Can you prove that your answer is correct? Prove that . . . Defend your answer. Show me how to solve that and explain what you are doing.

Key Points

♦ Concrete, pictorial and abstract
♦ Composing and decomposing numbers
♦ Expanding numbers
♦ Adding 10 to a number
♦ Adding 2- and 3-digit numbers
♦ Comparing numbers

Chapter Summary

It is important to spend time developing place value throughout the year. At the beginning of the year be sure to spend a bit of time reviewing the place value standards from second grade through energizers and routines. During the first week of school set up workstations to review the priority place value standards from the year before. Keep those workstations up all year and add the new ones as they are taught. Also be sure to make sure that parents understand what the place value standards are and ways that they can help to develop them.

Reflection Questions

1. How are you currently teaching place value lessons?
2. Are you making sure that you do concrete, pictorial and abstract activities?

3. What do your students struggle with the most and what ideas are you taking away from this chapter that might inform your work around those struggles?

References

Hanich, L., Jordan, N., Kaplan, D., & Dick, J. (2001). Performance across different areas of mathematical cognition in children with learning difficulties. *Journal of Educational Psychology*, *93*(3), 615.

Jordan, N. C., & Hanich, L. B. (2000). Mathematical thinking in second-grade children with different types of learning difficulties. *Journal of Learning Disabilities*, *33*, 567–578.

Kamii, C. (1985). Leading primary education toward excellence: Beyond worksheets and drill. *Young Children*, *40*(6), 3–9.

Kamii, C., & Joseph, L. (1988). Teaching place value and double-column addition. *Arithmetic Teacher*, *35*(6), 48–52.

Kentucky Department of Education. (2007). *Support materials for core content for assessment version 4.1 mathematics*. Retrieved January 15, 2017.

Miura, I., Okamoto, Y., Chungsoon, K., & Steere, M. (1993). First graders' cognitive representations of understanding of place value: Cross-national comparisons: France, Japan, Korea, Sweden, and the United States. *Journal of Educational Psychology*, *85*(1), 24–30.

Moeller, K., Pixner, S., Zuber, J., Kaufmann, L., & Nuerk, H. C. (2011). Early place-value understanding as a precursor for later arithmetic performance—a longitudinal study on numerical development. *Research in Developmental Disabilities*, *32*(5), 1837–1851.

National Council of Teachers of Mathematics (NCTM). (2000). *Principles and standards for school mathematics*. Reston, VA: NCTM.

National Council of Teachers of Mathematics (NCTM). (2006). *Curriculum focal points for prekindergarten through grade 8 mathematics: A quest for coherence*. Reston, VA: NCTM.

National Research Council. (2009). Mathematics learning in early childhood paths toward excellence and equity. In C. T. Cross, T. Woods, & H. Schweingruber (Eds.), *Committee on early childhood mathematics, center for education, division of behavioral and social sciences in education* (pp. 1–386). The National Academies Press.

Sherman, H. J., Richardson, L. I., & Yard, G. J. (2013). *Teaching learners who struggle with mathematics: Systematic intervention and remediation*. Boston, MA: Pearson.

Small, M. (2017). *Good questions: Great ways to differentiate math in the standards based classroom*. New York: Teachers College Press.

Webb, N. (2002). *An analysis of the alignment between mathematics standards and assessments for three states*. Paper presented at the annual meeting of the American Educational Research Association, New Orleans, LA.

8

Fraction Guided Math Lessons

Worldwide, students have trouble with fractions. Yet, fractions are foundational to understanding other aspects of mathematics. Researchers emphasize the key to getting students to understand fractions is to build on conceptual understanding. If students have conceptual understanding, then when they have to learn and use procedural knowledge it makes it that much easier because they understand what they are doing.

In the primary grades, the conceptual understanding foundation is being laid. In third grade there must be an emphasis on understanding fractions as equal sized pieces of a whole, plotting a fraction on a number line and beginning concepts of equivalence. When this emphasis is not placed on the teaching and learning of fractions, students walk away with misunderstandings and misconceptions that grow and impede the learning of more difficult fraction concepts. One of the biggest misconceptions that students carry with them is viewing the numerator and the denominator as separate numbers rather than 1 number.

Research shows that young children can understand basic fraction concepts such as sharing and the size of fractions when they are set in real-life contexts. Given real contexts, students can develop a fundamental understanding of ordering fractions and equivalence in third grade. It is very important to contextualize the discussion about fractions so that students have stories to understand the concepts. We must try to connect students "intuitive knowledge to formal fraction concepts" (Fazio & Siegler, n.d.).

It is also important to start introducing formal fraction names and attach them to the models and have students do drawings and sketches of these fractions with labels. Fraction notation is important and we don't want students to be afraid of it, so we should give them plenty of opportunities to write and name the fractions. We should spend a great deal of time building conceptual understanding by doing measurement activities, number lines and comparing activities based on real-life situations. We can use measuring string for jewelry making, talking about sharing food and using rulers.

Research Note

Students struggle with fractions. On a national test, only 50% of American eighth graders correctly ordered three fractions from smallest to largest (National Council of Teachers of Mathematics, 2007). Students confuse whole numbers and fractions and often assume what is true for whole numbers is true for fractions even through high school (Vamvakoussi & Vosniadou, 2010). Children should be introduced to fractions at an early age, making connections to their informal intuitive understanding of sharing and proportionality (Fazio & Siegler; Empson, 1999).

DOI: 10.4324/9781003169543-8

In this chapter, we will explore:

♦ Plotting fractions on a number line (see Figures 8.1 to 8.58)
♦ Fractions equivalent to 1 whole
♦ Comparing fractions
♦ Fractions as a set

Plotting Fractions on a Number Line

Overview

Figure 8.1 Overview

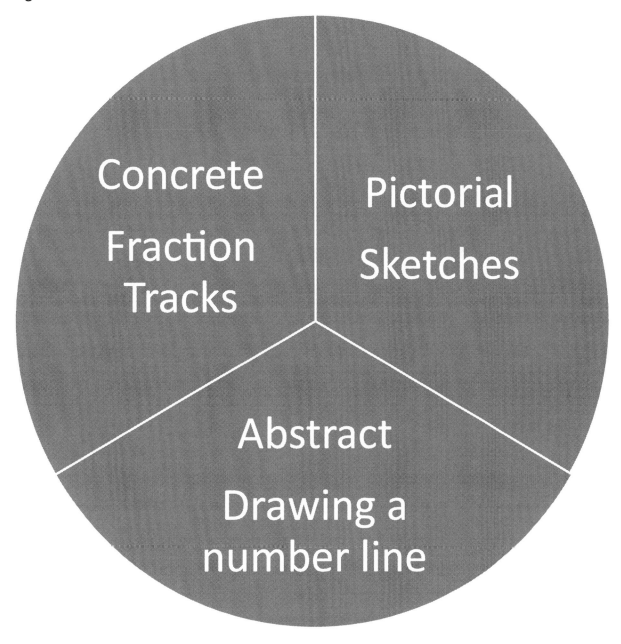

Figure 8.2 Planning Template

Fractions on a Number Line

Big Idea: Numbers, Comparison

Enduring Understanding: Students will understand that fractions are number on a number line

Essential Question: Why are fractions important? How do we use them in real life?

I can statement: I can plot a fraction on a number line.

Materials
- Tools: Fraction Strips
- Templates: Fraction Strip Template
- Crayons
- Paper

Cycle of Engagement

Concrete:

 (EAI)

Pictorial:

1 Whole			
½		½	
⅓	⅓		⅓
¼	¼	¼	¼

Abstract:

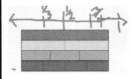

Vocabulary & Language Frames

Vocabulary: whole, halves, thirds, fourths, sixths, eighths, benchmark fraction, fraction

Math Talk:
___ is greater than ____
___ is less than___
____is a benchmark fraction

Math Processes/Practices
- Problem Solving
- Reasoning
- Models
- Tools
- Precision
- Structure
- Pattern

Figure 8.3 Differentiation

Three Differentiated Lessons		
In this series of lessons, students are working on plotting fractions on the number line. They are developing this concept through concrete activities, pictorial activities and abstract activities. Here are some things to think about as you do these lessons.		
Emerging	**On Grade Level**	**Above Grade Level**
Do a lot of work with students looking at fraction strips and where the fractions are on the number line.	Do a lot of work with different manipulatives and having the students do math sketches plotting fractions on a number line.	Work with more denominators.

 Looking for Misunderstandings and Common Errors

This is a tricky skill for many students. The way they learn is to work with manipulatives and discuss where these fractions would be plotted.

Figure 8.4 Anchor Chart

Fraction Strips

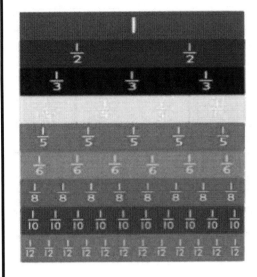

Fraction Strip Template

1 Whole			
½		½	
⅓	⅓		⅓
¼	¼	¼	¼

Abstract

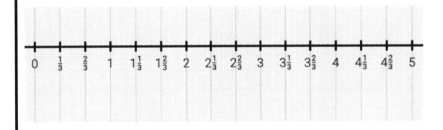

Concrete Lesson

Figure 8.5 Concrete Introduction

<table>
<tr>
<td colspan="2" align="center"><h2>Introduction to Fractions on a Number line</h2></td>
</tr>
<tr>
<td>Launch</td>
<td>

Teacher: Today we are going to work on using fraction strips to think about fractions on the number line.

Vocabulary: fractions, benchmark fractions, halves, thirds, fourths, whole

Math Talk:
_____ is greater than _____
_____ is less than _____
_____ is the same as _____

</td>
</tr>
<tr>
<td>Model</td>
<td>

Teacher: Here we are going to work with fraction strips. I just want you to tell me what you notice?

Katie: I notice that the first one is a whole.
Mark: The second one is cut in 2 pieces.
Terri: The third one is cut into 3 pieces.

Teacher: What is more, the ½ or 2 of the thirds?

</td>
</tr>
</table>

(Continued)

(Continued)

	Mary: Two-thirds is more.
	Teacher: So, if we are looking at this as a way to help us with our number line. The line at the top is the number line. We are going to the 2nd row where it is cut in 2 halves. So everybody draw a line at the top and draw where ½ would be. That is considered a benchmark number. It helps us know where we are on the number line. Let me see where everyone has marked ½. Look at your neighbor's. Does it look right? Everybody has ½?
Checking for Understanding	**Teacher:** Let me see where everyone has marked ½. Look at your neighbor's. Does it look right? Everybody has ½? Ok, we are going to keep going.

Figure 8.6 Student Activity

	Concrete Student Activity
Guided Practice/ Checking for Understanding	**Teacher:** Ok, where could we put a third, if we use our fraction strips to guide us? **Nekeli:** It's here. Where the first black one is. See, it would go here. **Teacher:** So, is a ⅓ before or after ½ on the number line. **Mike:** It's a 3 but it is before….(shakes his head) **Teacher:** Well let's look at the size. Is it bigger or smaller. **Mike:** A third is smaller. **Teacher:** So ⅓ is smaller. If the whole line is this, a small piece is a ⅓ but a bigger piece is a ½. So that half comes after because it is a bigger part of the number line.
Set up for Independent Practice	Every child gets to share out their thinking about plotting a fraction on the number line and how they reasoned about it. We are going to be talking more about this in the upcoming days. Are there any questions? What was interesting today? What was tricky?

Figure 8.7 Lesson Close

Close
• What did we do today?   • How did we model the math?   • Was this easy or tricky?   • Turn to a partner and state one thing you learned today.

Visual Lesson

Figure 8.8 Visual Introduction

<table>
<tr>
<td colspan="2"><h2 align="center">Introduction to Visual Explorations:</h2></td>
</tr>
<tr>
<td>Launch</td>
<td>Teacher: Today we are going to work on using fraction strip template to think about fractions on the number line.

Vocabulary: fractions, benchmark fractions, halves, thirds, fourths, whole

Math Talk:
_____ is greater than _____
_____ is less than _____
_____ is the same as _____</td>
</tr>
<tr>
<td>Model</td>
<td>Teacher: Let's look at the fraction strip template. Tell me what you notice?

Jennifer: I see that ½ is more than a ⅓.

Teacher: So, if we were to write that on the number line, who can show me what that should look like?

Jennifer: I would draw a line and cut it in half. Then, I would put ⅓ over here (she points to the left).

</td>
</tr>
<tr>
<td>Checking for Understanding</td>
<td>Teacher: I am going to give each one of you a problem. I want you to practice representing it with your sketches. Then, you will explain what you did. Who wants to go first?</td>
</tr>
</table>

Figure 8.9 Student Activity

Visual Student Activity	
Guided Practice/ Checking for Understanding	**Teacher:** Who wants to go next? **Ted:** I notice that ⅔ is more than ½. Teacher: Can you show that on the number line? **Ted:** Yes. See I put ½ here and then ⅔ over here (and he points to the right of ½). **Teacher:** How do you know that ⅔ is more than ½? **Ted:** Because it takes up more space.
Set up for Independent Practice	*Teacher gives everybody a chance to do and discuss a problem. After everyone has shared the lesson ends.* We are going to be talking more about that in the upcoming days. Are there any questions? What was interesting today? What was tricky?

Within the Guided Practice cell, a number line and a fraction bar diagram appear:

1 Whole			
½		½	
⅓	⅓		⅓
¼	¼	¼	¼

Figure 8.10 Lesson Close

Close
• What did we do today? • What was the math we were practicing? • How did we model the math? • Was this easy or tricky? • Turn to a partner and state one thing you learned today.

Figure 8.11 Fraction Strip Template

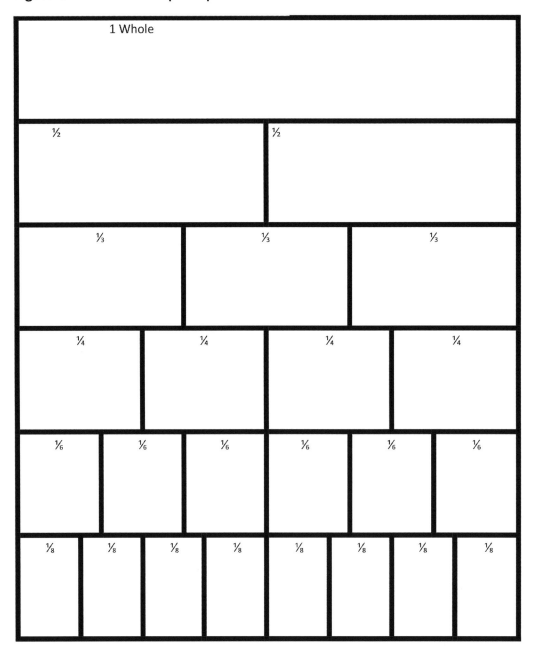

Abstract Lesson

Figure 8.12 Abstract Introduction

Introduction to Abstract Explorations

Launch	**Teacher:** Today we are going to work on using fraction strips to think about fractions on the number line. **Vocabulary**: fractions, benchmark fractions, halves, thirds, fourths, whole **Math Talk:** _____ is greater than _____ _____ is less than _____ _____ is the same as _____
Model	Today we are going to look at how we can use our fraction strips to help us reason about about where fractions go on the number line. So I am going to have you lay down your fraction strips and then plot some of the fraction using them as a guide. See here, I knew where half was and now I can see that ⅓ is smaller than ½ and ⅔ is greater than ½. 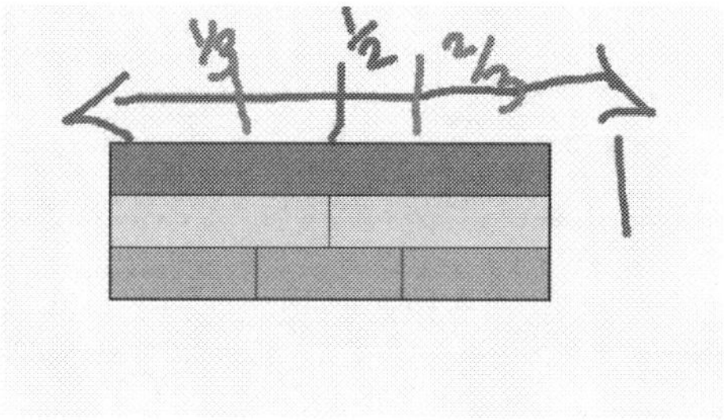
Checking for Understanding	The first thing I want you to do is to plot ⅓, ¾ and ½ on the number line. **Joe:** I see that ⅓ is smaller than ½ and ¾ is larger than ½. 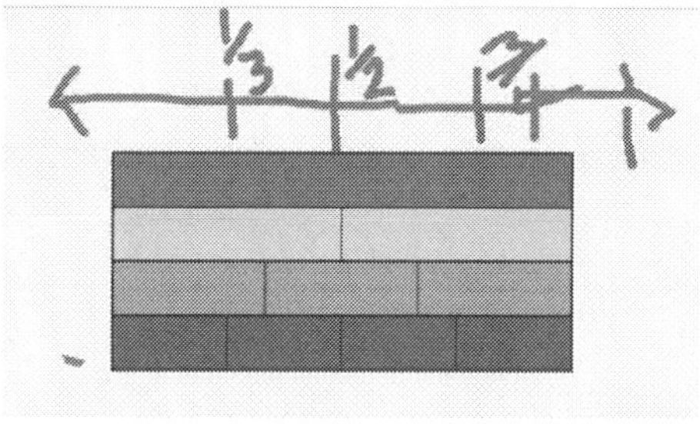

Figure 8.13 Student Activity

Abstract Student Activity

Guided Practice/ Checking for Understanding	**Marta:** I drew a number line using my fraction strips. I put ½. I can see that ½ is bigger than ¼. I can see that ⅔ is more than ½. 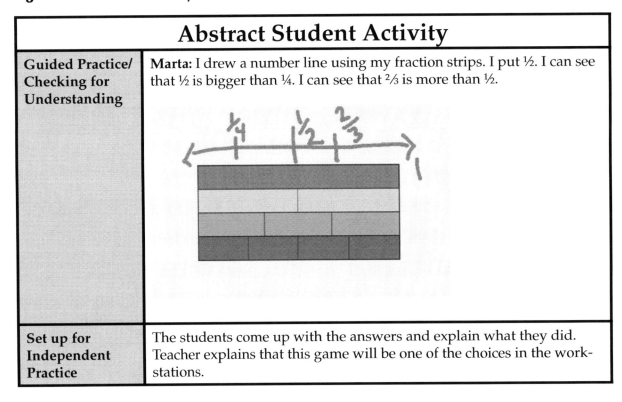
Set up for Independent Practice	The students come up with the answers and explain what they did. Teacher explains that this game will be one of the choices in the workstations.

Figure 8.14 Lesson Close

Close

- What did we do today?
- What was the math we were practicing?
- How did we model the math?
- Was this easy or tricky?
- Turn to a partner and state one thing you learned today.

Section Summary

Students have many problems learning to plot numbers on a number line. This work should be scaffolded with manipulatives. You should have students work first with ½ as a benchmark number. Then have students notice where 1 is and where ½ is. Then, have them locate a fraction that is greater than 1. Then have students start locating fractions that are less than 1. Scaffold the work so that students get comfortable with the idea of the reiteration of the unit fraction so that they understand ⁴⁄₃ as 1 more third than ³⁄₃. We want them to be able to reason about the size of fractions, and given that size where they should be on the number line.

Fractions Equivalent to 1 Whole

Overview

Figure 8.15 Overview

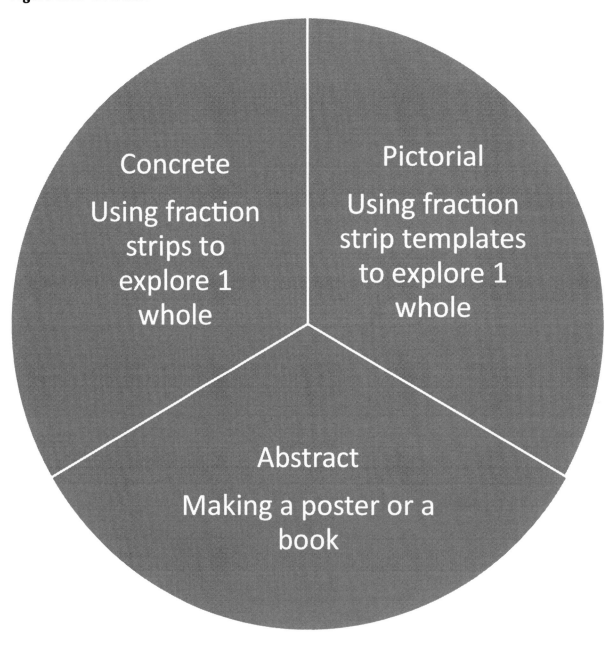

Figure 8.16 Planning Template

Fractions as a Whole

Big Idea: Numbers, Equivalence **Enduring Understanding:** Students will understand equivalence of unit fractions as a whole. **Essential Question:** Why are fractions important? How do we use them in real life? **I can statement:** I can discuss and model fractions as whole units.	**Materials** • Tools: Fraction Strips • Templates: Fraction Strip Template • Crayons • Paper

Cycle of Engagement

Concrete:

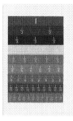
(EAI)

Pictorial:

1 Whole			
½		½	
⅓	⅓		⅓
¼	¼	¼	¼

Abstract:

Vocabulary & Language Frames

Vocabulary: whole, halves, thirds, fourths, sixths, eighths

Math Talk:
___ is greater than ____
___ is less than___
___ is equal to _____

Math Processes/Practices
• **Problem Solving**
• **Reasoning**
• **Models**
• **Tools**
• **Precision**
• **Structure**
• **Pattern**

Figure 8.17 Differentiation

Three Differentiated Lessons		
In this series of lessons, students are working on understanding fractions as a whole number. They are developing this concept through concrete activities, pictorial activities and abstract activities. Here are some things to think about as you do these lessons.		
Emerging	**On Grade Level**	**Above Grade Level**
Students should work with different models, including fraction circles, squares and strips.	Students should use models to understand how to fractions make wholes.	Students should work with larger denominators.
Looking for Misunderstandings and Common Errors		
Students have trouble understanding the iteration of a unit fraction. Use manipulatives to reinforce this concept. Be sure to use playdoh because the kinesthetic aspect of cutting the pieces is really good. Also, have students work with measurement and fractions.		

Figure 8.18 Anchor Chart

Concrete
(EAI)

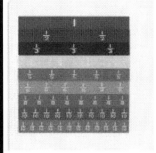

Pictorial

1 Whole			
½		½	
⅓	⅓		⅓
¼	¼	¼	¼

Abstract

- $\frac{2}{2} = 1$

- $\frac{3}{3} = 1$

- $\frac{4}{4} = 1$

- $\frac{6}{6} = 1$

- $\frac{8}{8} = 1$

Concrete Lesson

Figure 8.19 Concrete Introduction

Introduction to Concrete Explorations

Launch	**Teacher:** Today we are going to work on using fraction strips to think about fractions **that are the same.** **Vocabulary:** fractions, benchmark fractions, halves, thirds, fourths, whole, equivalent **Math Talk:** _____ is greater than _____ _____ is less than _____ _____ is the same as _____
Model	**Teacher:** Here we are going to work with fraction strips. I just want you to tell me what you notice that is the same? **Katie:** I notice that the first one is a whole. **Mark:** Two twos is the same as 1. **Terri:** We call those halves. We can say 2 halves is equal to 1 whole. **Kenny:** I see that 3 thirds is equal to 1 whole to. **Mary:** I see that 4 fourths is equal to 1 whole to. **Teacher:** Is there some sort of pattern? **Mary:** I bet that 5 fifths is 1 whole too. **Teacher:** I bet you are correct.
Checking for Understanding	**Teacher:** Ok. We are going to explore some more fractions.

Figure 8.20 Student Activity

	Concrete Student Activity
Guided Practice/ Checking for Understanding	**Teacher:** So, look at the other fractions on your fraction templates and tell me what you notice. **Jamal:** I see that 6/6 makes 1 whole. **Terri:** I see that 8/8 makes 1 whole. **Teacher:** So, the pattern continues. We can say that if you have all the pieces, then you have a whole.
Set up for Independent Practice	**Teacher:** We are going to be talking more about this in the upcoming days. Are there any questions? What was interesting today? What was tricky?

Figure 8.21 Lesson Close

Close
• What did we do today? • What was the math we were practicing? • How did we model the math? • Was this easy or tricky? • Turn to a partner and state one thing you learned today.

Visual Lesson

Figure 8.22 Visual Introduction

Introduction to Visual Explorations

Launch	**Teacher:** Today we are going to work on using fraction strips to think about fractions that are the same. **Vocabulary:** fractions, benchmark fractions, halves, thirds, fourths, whole, equivalent **Math Talk:** ____ is greater than _____ ____ is less than _____ ____ is the same as _____
Model	**Teacher:** Today we are going to do what we did yesterday but we are going to look at it and color it on our template. Who can tell me what $^3/_3$ is equivalent to? **Tim:** 3 thirds is equal to 1 whole. See, 1,2,3 and that is as long as 1 whole. **Kimmy:** 4 fourths is equal to 1 whole too. See 1,2,3,4 and that is as long as 1 whole.

1 Whole			
½		½	
⅓	⅓		⅓
¼	¼	¼	¼

|
| **Checking for Understanding** | **Jack:** I know one. 2 halves are also equal to 1 whole!

1 Whole			
½		½	
⅓	⅓		⅓
¼	¼	¼	¼

Teacher: Yes. Now we are going to make a poster to show all of this. Each part will discuss different fractions that are equivalent to 1 whole. |

Figure 8.23 Student Activity

	Visual Student Activity
Guided Practice/ Checking for Understanding	**Tami:** 6 sixths is equal to 1 whole.

1 Whole							
½				½			
⅓		⅓			⅓		
¼		¼		¼		¼	
⅙	⅙	⅙	⅙	⅙	⅙		
⅛	⅛	⅛	⅛	⅛	⅛	⅛	⅛

Set up for Independent Practice	After all the students share, the teacher wraps up the lesson and the students go to their workstations.

Figure 8.24 Lesson Close

Close
• What did we do today?   • What was the math we were practicing?   • How did we model the math?   • Was this easy or tricky?   • Turn to a partner and state one thing you learned today.

Abstract Lesson

Figure 8.25 Abstract Introduction

	Introduction to Abstract Explorations
Launch	**Teacher:** Today we are going to work on using fraction strips to think about fractions that are the same. **Vocabulary:** fractions, benchmark fractions, halves, thirds, fourths, whole, equivalent **Math Talk:** ____ is greater than _____ ____ is less than _____ ____ is the same as _____
Model	**Teacher:** Today I want you to make a poster or a book to show fractions that equal 1. Each part will discuss different fractions that are equivalent to 1 whole. **Kelli:** I am going to make a poster. **Todd:** I want to make a book. **Mary:** I am going to make a poster. **Teacher:** Ok, here is what your project must show. You must have these parts: A section talking about how many halves make a whole. A section talking about how many thirds make a whole. A section talking about how many fourths make a whole. A section talking about how many sixths make a whole. A section talking about how many eighths make a whole. Here is a checklist so you can make sure you have all the parts. Here is the paper if you want to make a poster. Here is a booklet if you want to make a book. Here are the templates.

	Checklist for Fraction Project	
	I made a _____.	
	Section	I did it
	Halves	
	Thirds	
	Fourths	
	Sixths	
	Eighths	
Checking for Understanding	**Teacher:** Does everybody understand what we are going to do?	

Figure 8.26 Student Activity

Visual Student Activities	
Guided Practice/ Checking for Understanding	After the students have gotten started, the teacher goes around and asks each one of them questions about their work. **Teacher:** Terri what are you doing? **Terri:** I drew 3 thirds to show how it makes a whole. See….
Set up for Independent Practice	Every child shares out some of their work. **Teacher:** We are going to be talking more about that in the upcoming days. Are there any questions? What was interesting today? What was tricky?

Figure 8.27 Lesson Close

Close
• What did we do today?
• What was the math we were practicing?
• How did we model the math?
• Was this easy or tricky?
• Turn to a partner and state one thing you learned today.

Section Summary

Getting students to understand the equivalence of fractions to a whole takes a great deal of exploration. Students should explore this concept with fraction strips, squares and circles. They should do it with both marked and unmarked manipulatives. It is important that they can build it, draw it and then explain it.

Comparing Fractions

Overview

Figure 8.28 Overview

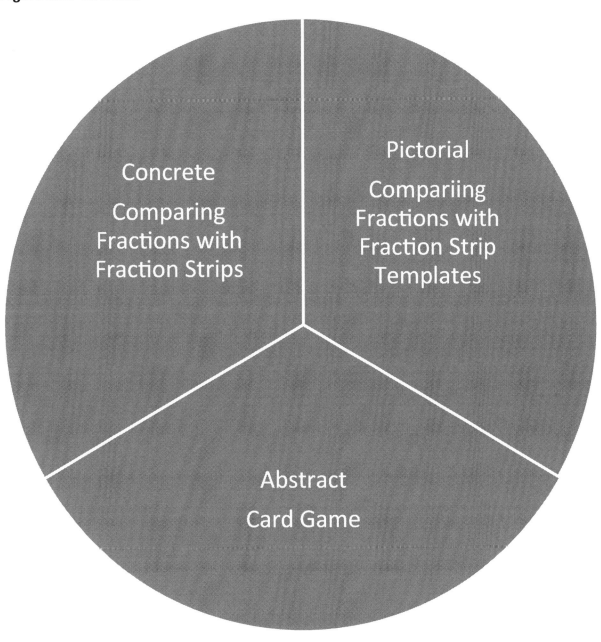

Figure 8.29 Planning Template

Fractions as a Whole	
Big Idea: Numbers **Enduring Understanding:** Students will understand that we can compare fractions that have the same size whole. **Essential Question:** Why are fractions important? How do we use them in real life? **I can statement:** I can discuss and compare fractions.	**Materials** • Tools: Fraction Strips • Templates: Fraction Strip Template • Crayons • Paper
Cycle of Engagement **Concrete:** (EAI) **Pictorial:**	**Vocabulary & Language Frames** **Vocabulary:** whole, halves, thirds, fourths, sixths, eighths **Math Talk:** ____ is greater than _____ ____ is less than____ ____ is equal to _____

<table>
<tr><td colspan="12">1 Whole</td></tr>
<tr><td colspan="6">½</td><td colspan="6">½</td></tr>
<tr><td colspan="4">⅓</td><td colspan="4">⅓</td><td colspan="4">⅓</td></tr>
<tr><td colspan="3">¼</td><td colspan="3">¼</td><td colspan="3">¼</td><td colspan="3">¼</td></tr>
</table>

Abstract:
²∕₃ **is more than** ¹∕₆
²∕₃ > ¹∕₆

Math Processes/Practices
• **Problem Solving**
• **Reasoning**
• **Models**
• **Tools**
• **Precision**
• **Structure**
• **Pattern**

Figure 8.30 Differentiation

Three Differentiated Lessons		
In this series of lessons, students are working on the concept of comparing fractions. They are developing this concept through concrete activities, pictorial activities and abstract activities. Here are some things to think about as you do these lessons.		
Emerging	**On Grade Level**	**Above Grade Level**
Students should work with manipulatives to compare fractions. I would begin by having them work with halves, thirds and fourths.	Students work with specific denominators in most states: halves, fourths, eighths, thirds and sixths.	Students should work with the fourth grade denominators as well.

 Looking for Misunderstandings and Common Errors

Students have a lot of trouble comparing fractions. They get very confused by looking at the numbers in fractions and then interpreting them as whole numbers so they will say things like $\frac{1}{3}$ is greater than $\frac{1}{2}$ because 3 is more than 2. Telling stories where they have to reason about the size of fractions helps them to reason. For example, using the fraction strips you should ask if I had a candy bar and I said you can have $\frac{1}{2}$ or $\frac{1}{3}$ of my candy bar, which fraction of my candy bar would you want and why?

Figure 8.31 Anchor Chart

Pictorial

$\frac{1}{2}$		$\frac{1}{2}$	
$\frac{1}{4}$	$\frac{1}{4}$	$\frac{1}{4}$	$\frac{1}{4}$

Concrete

Abstract

$\frac{5}{3}$ is more than $\frac{5}{6}$

$\frac{5}{3} > \frac{5}{6}$

Concrete Lesson

Figure 8.32 Concrete Introduction

Introduction to Concrete Explorations

Launch	**Teacher:** Today we are going to work on using fraction strip template to compare fractions.
	Vocabulary: fractions, benchmark fractions, halves, thirds, fourths, whole
	Math Talk: _____ is greater than _____ _____ is less than _____ _____ is the same as _____
	Teacher: Let's look at the fraction strip template. Tell me what you notice about the size of the fractions?
Model	**Teacher:** Let's look at the fraction strip template. Tell me what you notice about the size of the fractions?

Teacher: Let's use ½ as our benchmark fraction. We will compare some other fractions to it today. What do you notice?

Yesenia: I see that 2 thirds is more than ½.
Todd: I see that 8 eighths is bigger than half.
Clint: I see that ¾ is bigger than half.

Teacher: What are some fractions that are smaller than ½?

Marta: ⅓ is smaller than ½.
Teddy: ¼ is smaller than ½.
Mike: ⅛ is smaller than ½.

Checking for Understanding	*Teacher reads 2 more problems that the group discusses.*
	Teacher: Ok. I am going to give each one of you your own problem. I want you to read it. Solve it. Be ready to share how you did it. I am going to watch you and if you need help, look at our anchor charts and of course you can ask me.

Figure 8.33 Student Activity

	Concrete Student Activities
Guided Practice/ Checking for Understanding	Teacher: What are some fractions that are the same as half? Marta: I see 2 fourths is equivalent to ½. Teddy: I see that 3 sixths is equivalent to ½. Clint: I see 4 eighths is equivalent to ½. 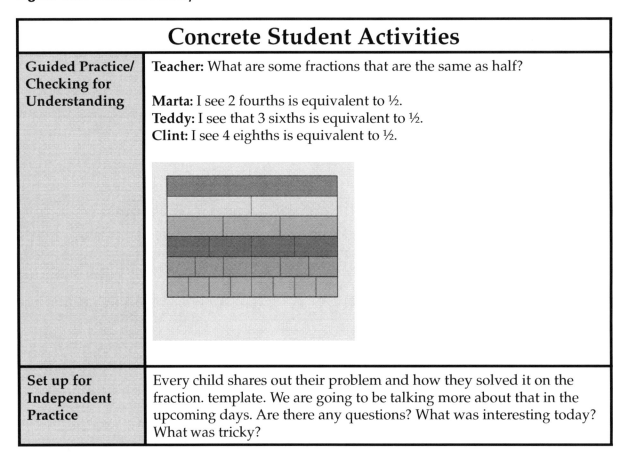
Set up for Independent Practice	Every child shares out their problem and how they solved it on the fraction. template. We are going to be talking more about that in the upcoming days. Are there any questions? What was interesting today? What was tricky?

Figure 8.34 Lesson Close

Close
• What did we do today? • What was the math we were practicing? • What were we doing with our tools today? • Was this easy or tricky? • Turn to a partner and state one thing you learned today.

Visual Lesson

Figure 8.35 Visual Introduction

Introduction to a Visual Explorations

Launch	**Teacher:** Today we are going to work on using the fraction strip template to think about fractions on the number line. **Vocabulary:** fractions, benchmark fractions, halves, thirds, fourths, whole **Math Talk:** _____ is greater than _____ _____ is less than _____ _____ is the same as _____ **Teacher:** Let's look at the fraction strip template. Tell me what you notice about the size of the fractions?
Model	**Teacher:** Today we are going to play a fraction game where you compare them. Each partner will pull a card and whoever has the larger fraction will win the cards. Remember the fractions have to be the same size to compare them. Let's have look. **Harry:** I have $4/6$. 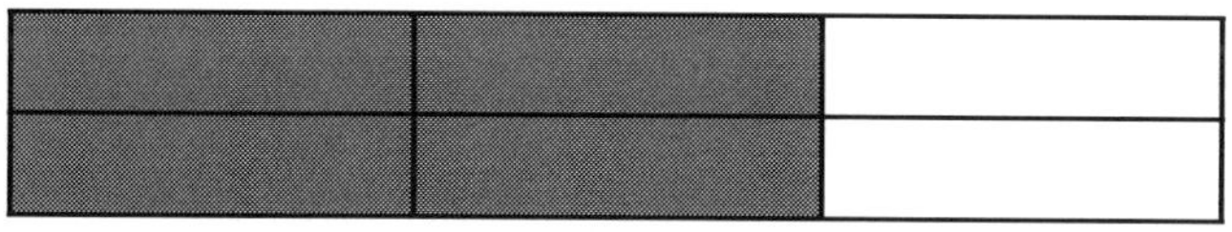 **Kate:** I have $5/6$. I have more. 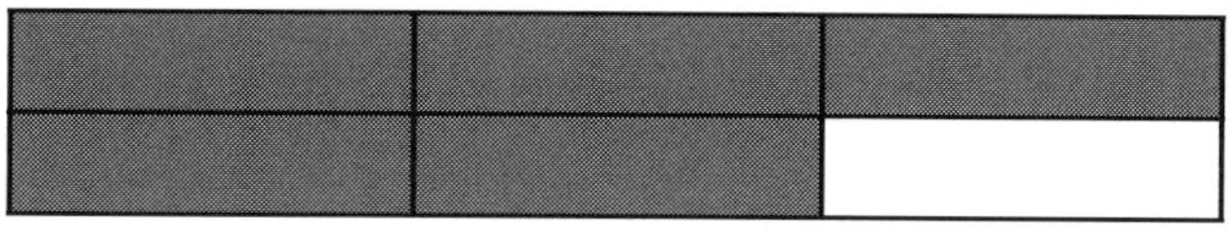
Checking for Understanding	**Teddy:** I have $6/6$. I have more. I have 1 whole. 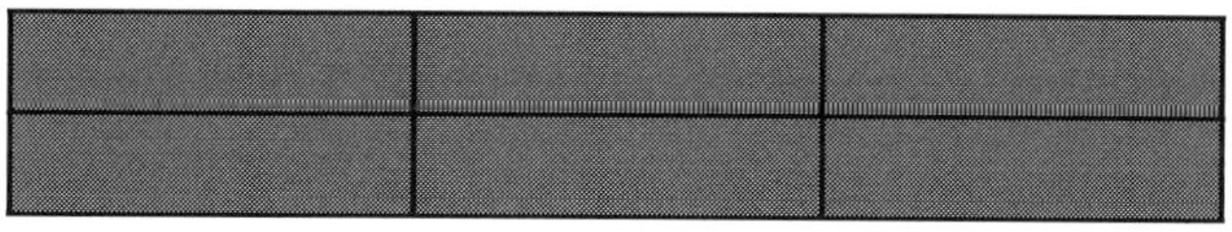 **Kelli:** I have $3/6$. 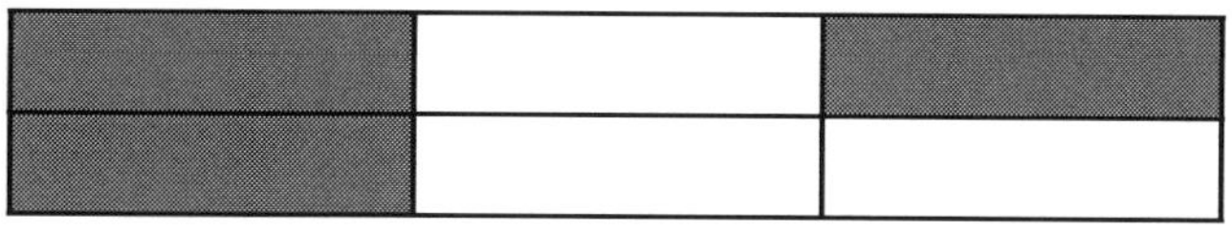 **Teacher:** Ok, I am going to give each of you a baggie with the game cards and you can compare them.

Figure 8.36 Student Activity

Visual Student Activity	
Guided Practice/ Checking for Understanding	Teacher watches the students play the game and asks them questions. **Teacher: Grace and Tami tell me about this round.** **Grace:** I have $^0/_6$. 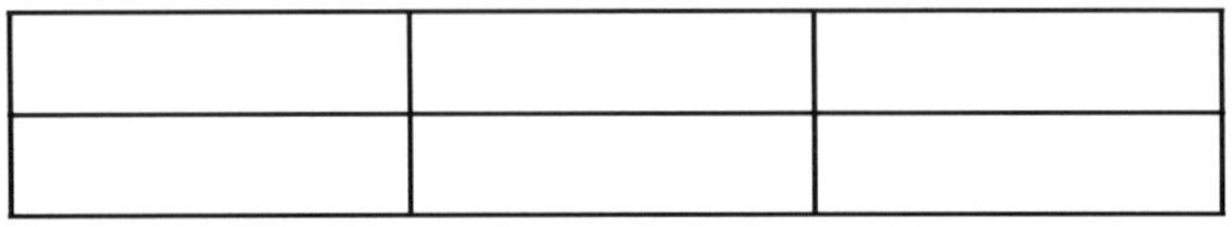 _(blank 2×3 grid)_ **Tami:** I have $^2/_6$. I have more.  _(2×3 grid with top-left two cells shaded)_
Set up for Independent Practice	_Teacher gives everybody a chance to do and discuss a problem. After everyone has shared the lesson ends._ _**Teacher:** We are going to be talking more about this in the upcoming days. Are there any questions? What was interesting today? What was tricky?_

Figure 8.37 Lesson Close

Close
• What did we do today? • What was the math we were practicing? • How did we model the math? • Was this easy or tricky? • Turn to a partner and state one thing you learned today.

Figure 8.38 Compare Game Cards

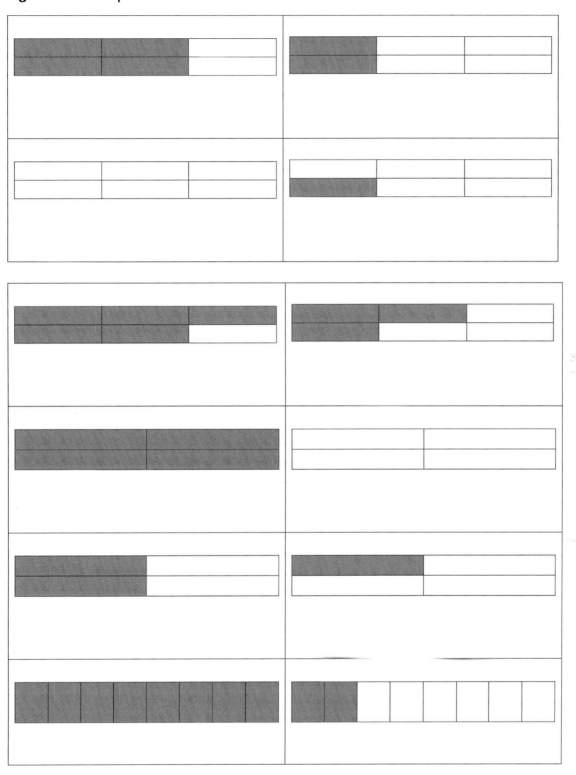

Abstract Lesson

Figure 8.39 Abstract Introduction

<table>
<tr>
<td colspan="2" align="center"><h2>Introduction to Abstract Lesson</h2></td>
</tr>
<tr>
<td>Launch</td>
<td>

Teacher: Today we are going to work on comparing fractions with just the numbers. You can look at your fraction strip template if you get stuck.

Vocabulary: fractions, benchmark fractions, halves, thirds, fourths, whole

Math Talk:
____ is greater than _____
____ is less than _____
____ is the same as _____

</td>
</tr>
<tr>
<td>Model</td>
<td>

Teacher: Today we are going to play a fraction game where you compare them. Each partner will pull a card and whoever has the larger fraction will win the cards.

½	¾

²/₆	⁴/₈

³/₆	²/₃

</td>
</tr>
<tr>
<td>Checking for Understanding</td>
<td>

Teacher: Who wants to do a round?

Yesenia: I got ²/₃ and that is more.

²/₃	⁴/₈

Maite: I know this because ⁴/₈ is the same as half. ²/₃ is more than half.

</td>
</tr>
</table>

Figure 8.40 Student Activity

	Abstract Student Activity
Guided Practice/ Checking for Understanding	**Teacher:** Who wants to do a round? **Yasmin:** I got $\frac{1}{6}$ and that is less than $\frac{5}{5}$. $\boxed{\frac{2}{3}}$ $\boxed{\frac{5}{5}}$ **Mark:** I know this because $\frac{5}{5}$ is the whole and $\frac{2}{3}$ is less than a whole. You need $\frac{3}{3}$ to have another whole.
Set up for Independent Practice	The teacher watches, listens to and takes notes on the students as they play. She notes who needs more help, who is using the tools and which ones. Then she wraps up the lesson and sends the students to their workstations.

Figure 8.41 Lesson Close

Close
• What did we do today? • What was the math we were practicing? • What were we doing with our tools? • Was this easy or tricky? • Turn to a partner and state one thing you learned today.

Figure 8.42 Cards

$\frac{1}{2}$	1 whole	$\frac{2}{2}$
$\frac{1}{3}$	$\frac{1}{4}$	$\frac{1}{6}$
$\frac{2}{3}$	$\frac{2}{4}$	$\frac{2}{6}$
$\frac{3}{3}$	$\frac{3}{4}$	$\frac{3}{6}$
$\frac{1}{8}$	$\frac{4}{4}$	$\frac{4}{6}$
$\frac{0}{2}$	$\frac{0}{6}$	$\frac{5}{6}$
$\frac{2}{8}$	$\frac{4}{8}$	$\frac{6}{8}$
$\frac{3}{8}$	$\frac{5}{8}$	$\frac{7}{8}$

Section Summary

Comparing fractions can be tricky for students. They need a great deal of work with manipulatives to be able to internalize this and do it on their mental number line and depend on visualization. If they have had a great deal of experiences working with fraction bars, squares and circles, both concrete and paper, then they can visualize quite easily about the size of these fractions. Don't rush this; instead, leave this up as a center during the rest of the year, once you have taught fractions. This should be a part of the "hot topics" center.

Fractions as a Set

Overview

Figure 8.43 Overview

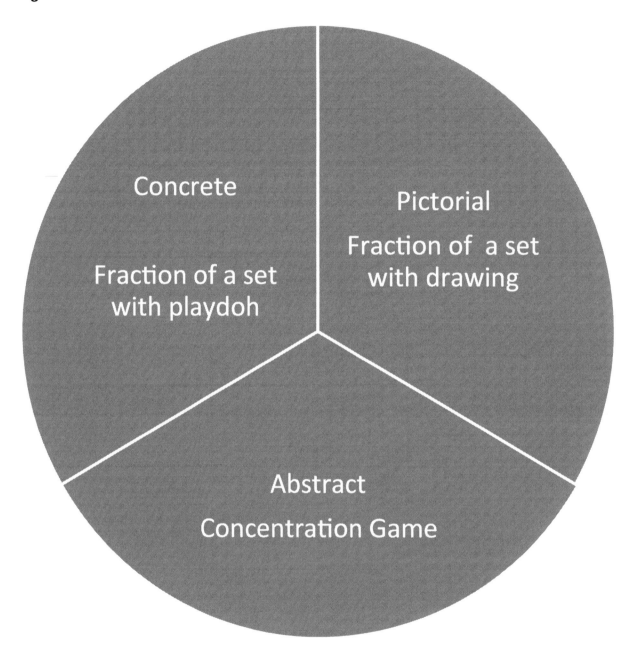

Figure 8.44 Planning Template

Fractions as a Set	
Big Idea: Numbers **Enduring Understanding:** Students will understand the idea of a fraction as a set **Essential Question:** Why are fractions important? How do we use them in real life? **I can statement:** I can discuss and model fractions as a set	**Materials** • Fraction Match Cards

Cycle of Engagement

Concrete:

Pictorial:

Abstract:
⅙ of this set is giraffes.

Vocabulary & Language Frames

Vocabulary: whole, halves, thirds, fourths, sixths, eighths

Math Talk:
The fraction of the set is _____
_____ is the fraction of this set

Math Processes/Practices
• **Problem Solving**
• **Reasoning**
• **Models**
• **Tools**
• **Precision**
• **Structure**
• **Pattern**

Figure 8.45 Differentiation

Three Differentiated Lessons		
In this series of lessons, students are working on the concept of a fraction of a set. Students should work on this concept through concrete activities, pictorial activities and abstract activities. Here are some things to think about as you do these lessons.		
Emerging	**On Grade Level**	**Above Grade Level**
Only a few states officially teach fraction of a set in third grade. However, many people informally teach it. Students get this concept fairly easily.	Students should be able to identify fractions of a set for designated denominators (usually halves, fourths, thirds, sixths and eighths).	Expand the range of denominators.
Looking for Misunderstandings and Common Errors		
Students understand this concept fairly easily. Be sure to have them explain their thinking when they are describing the fraction of the set they are talking about. For example, they could say, " $\frac{1}{3}$ of the set is zebras and $\frac{2}{3}$ of the set is hippos."		

Figure 8.46 Anchor Chart

Concrete:

Pictorial:

Abstract:

⅜ of this set is hippos. ⅝ of the set is zebras.

Concrete Lesson

Figure 8.47 Concrete Introduction

<div align="center">**Introduction to Concrete Explorations** *I am learning to compare numbers*</div>	
Launch	**Teacher:** Today we are going to work on finding a fraction of a set. **Vocabulary:** fractions, benchmark fractions, halves, thirds, fourths, whole **Math Talk:** _____ **is a fraction of this set.**
Model	**Teacher:** Today we are going to use our playdoh to look at the idea of a fraction being part of a set. Let's all roll 3 balls. So, we have 3 balls. We have $^3\!/_3$ of a set. When I say smash it, I want you to smash $^2\!/_3$ of the set. **Teacher:** Ok, let's roll 3 balls again. Now, we are going to smash $^1\!/_3$ of the set. Ok, now let's make 4 balls. What part of the set do we have? **Taylor:** We have 4 fourths of a set.
Checking for Understanding	**Teacher:**.. Somebody smash some and tell us what fraction of the set you have smashed. **Jorge:** I smashed 2 fourths of the set. Teacher goes around and each child gets to tell a story. Ok, now I am going to give you some smash it cards and you will work on your problems with your playdoh.

Figure 8.48 Student Activity

	Concrete Student Activity
Guided Practice/ Checking for Understanding	**Teacher:** Ok, now make 6 balls again. Somebody smash some and tell us what fraction of the set you have smashed. **Jorge:** I smashed 6 sixths of the set. I smashed the whole set. 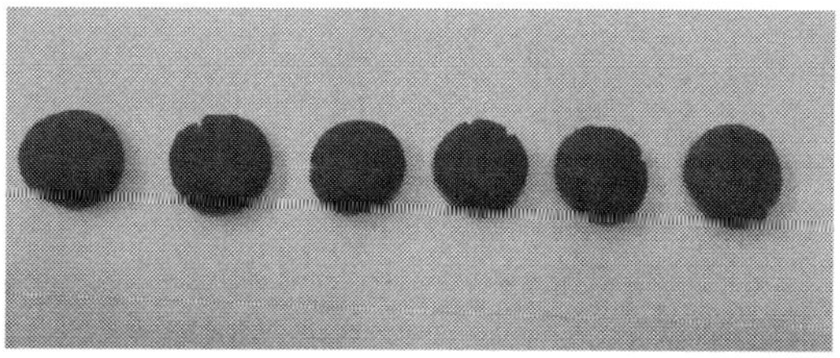 **Tami:** I smashed 2 sixths of the set. 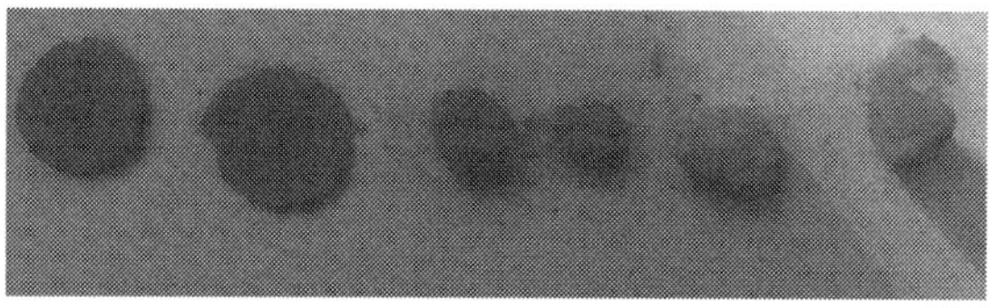
Set up for Independent Practice	Every child shares out their problem and how they solved it. We are going to be talking more about that in the upcoming days. Are there any questions? What was interesting today? What was tricky?

Figure 8.49 Lesson Close

Close
• What did we do today? • What was the math we were practicing? • How did we model the math? • Was this easy or tricky? • Turn to a partner and state one thing you learned today.

Figure 8.50 Smashing Part of a Set Cards

Smash $^2/_6$ of a set	Smash $^2/_6$ of a set
Smash $^1/_6$ of a set	Smash $^0/_6$ of a set
Smash $^2/_3$ of a set	Smash $^1/_3$ of a set
Smash $^2/_4$ of a set	Smash $^2/_4$ of a set
Smash $^3/_6$ of a set	Smash $^1/_4$ of a set

Smash $^2/_8$ of a set	Smash $^6/_8$ of a set
Smash $^1/_8$ of a set	Smash $^7/_8$ of a set
Smash $^3/_8$ of a set	Smash $^3/_3$ of a set
Smash $^4/_8$ of a set	Smash $^1/_2$ of a set of 4
Smash $^5/_8$ of a set	Smash $^0/_3$ of a set

Visual Lesson

Figure 8.51 Visual Introduction

	## Introduction to a Visual Exploration
Launch	**Teacher:** Today we are going to work on finding a fraction of a set. **Vocabulary:** fractions, benchmark fractions, halves, thirds, fourths, whole **Math Talk:** _____ **is a fraction of this set.**
Model	**Teacher:** Today we are going to draw a set and cross out a fraction of it. You will pull a card and then draw out the problem. A. Draw 3 circles. Cross out ⅔ of your set. Recording sheet
Checking for Understanding	B. Draw 4 circles. Cross out ²⁄₄ of your set. Recording sheet Students go around and pull a card and do a math sketch.

Figure 8.52 Student Activity

	Visual Student Activity
Guided Practice/ Checking for Understanding	You will pull a card and then draw out the problem. A. Draw 8 circles. Cross out $^2/_8$ of your set. **Recording sheet** (drawing of circles)
Set up for Independent Practice	*Teacher gives everybody a chance to do and discuss a problem. After everyone has shared the lesson ends.* We are going to be talking more about that in the upcoming days. Are there any questions? What was interesting today? What was tricky?

Figure 8.53 Lesson Close

Close
• What did we do today? • What was the math we were practicing? • How did we model the math? • Was this easy or tricky? • Turn to a partner and state one thing you learned today.

Abstract Lesson

Figure 8.54 Abstract Introduction

	Introduction to Abstract Explorations
Launch	**Teacher:** Today we are going to work on finding a fraction of a set. **Vocabulary**: fractions, benchmark fractions, halves, thirds, fourths, whole **Math Talk:** _____ **is a fraction of this set.**
Model	**Teacher:** Today we are going to play a concentration game. You guys know how to do that. In this game we are looking to match the numbers with the pictures. You are going to work with your partner to find all the matches. For example, this picture shows half of this set of animals is hippos. It also shows half of this set if giraffes. So if you flip these 2 cards you just have to describe how to use that fraction to talk about the set. **Teacher:** Juan describe how these cards go together. **Juan:** $2/3$ of this set is hippos.
Checking for Understanding	**Teacher:** Any questions? Ok, let's get started then.

Figure 8.55 Student Activity

	Abstract Student Activity
Guided Practice/ Checking for Understanding	*As the students play with their partners, the teacher watches, notices, takes notes and asks questions.* **Teacher:** Jamal and Claire tell me about your cards. **Juan:** $3/3$ of this set is hippos. **Claire:** The whole set is hippos. 
Set up for Independent Practice	The teacher continues to ask the students questions about their work as they do the activity. Afterwards, the students go to their workstations.

Figure 8.56 Lesson Close

Close
• What did we do today? • What was the math we were practicing? • Was this easy or tricky? • Turn to a partner and state one thing you learned today.

Section Summary

Working with fractions of sets is fairly easy for most children. This should be done first with concrete explorations and then drawings. Eventually students should work on describing and writing about fractions of a set. They should also get plenty of opportunities to create their own sets with things around the room, things they bring in from home and stickers. I find that stickers is a great activity because you can get tons of them for cheap, especially at the dollar store and then students can just go for it and create tons of sets and describe them.

Depth of Knowledge

Depth of Knowledge is a framework that encourages us to ask questions that require that students think, reason, explain, defend and justify their thinking (Webb, 2002). Here is a snapshot of what that can look like in terms of place value work.

Figure 8.57 DOK Activities

	What are different ways to learn to plot a fraction on a number line?	What are different ways to name a fraction as a whole?	What are different ways to compare fractions?	What are different ways to describe a fraction of a set?
DOK Level 1 (These are questions where students are required to simply recall/ reproduce an answer/do a procedure.)	Plot ½ on the number line	What does ⅔ mean?	Which is bigger, ½ or ⅓?	Name the fraction of this set
DOK Level 2 (These are questions where students have to use information, think about concepts and reason.) This is considered a more challenging problem than a level 1 problem.	Plot ⅔, ¼ and ½ on the number line. Explain what you did.	How do you know that ⁴⁄₄ is equivalent to 1 whole? Explain your thinking.	Compare ⅓ and ⅙. Explain your thinking.	Describe what a fraction of a set means. Give an example.
DOK Level 3 (These are questions where students have to reason, plan, explain, justify and defend their thinking.)	Plot 4 fractions on the number line from least to greatest. Explain what you did and defend your thinking with numbers, words and pictures.	How do you know that ⁸⁄₈ is equivalent to 1 whole? Explain what you did and defend your thinking with numbers, words and pictures. Tell me about how certain fractions can be equivalent to whole numbers.	Compare ⅓ and ⅙. Explain what you did and defend your thinking with numbers, words and pictures. Pick 2 fractions and compare them. Explain what you did and defend your thinking with numbers, words and pictures.	Name a fraction of a set. Show it in more than one way. Explain what you did and defend your thinking with numbers, words and pictures.

Adapted from Kaplinsky (https://robertkaplinsky.com/depth-knowledge-matrix-elementary-math/). A great resource for asking open questions is Marion Small's *Good Questions: Great ways to differentiate mathematics instruction in the stand-ards-based classroom* (2017).

Also, Robert Kaplinsky has done a great job in pushing our thinking forward with the Depth of Knowledge Matrices he created. Kentucky Dept. of Education also has great DOK Matrices (2007).

Figure 8.58 Asking Rigorous Questions

DOK 1	DOK 2 **At this level students explain their thinking.**	DOK 3 **At this level students have to justify, defend and prove their thinking with objects, drawings and diagrams.**
What is the answer to ??? Can you model the number? Can you model the problem? Can you identify the answer that matches this equation? How many hundreds, tens and ones are in this number?	How do you know that the equation is correct? Can you pick the correct answer and explain why it is correct? How can you model that problem? What is another way to model that problem? Can you model that on the . . . ??? Give me an example of a . . . type of problem. Which answer is incorrect? Explain your thinking	Can you prove that your answer is correct? Prove that . . . Defend your answer. Show me how to solve that and explain what you are doing.

Key Points

♦ Plotting fractions on a number line
♦ Naming a fraction as a whole number
♦ Comparing fractions
♦ Naming a fraction of a set

Chapter Summary

Teaching third grade students about fractions is very important. The work starts in the lower elementary grades, but it is much more formal in third grade. For students to really grasp the topics they must be introduced at the concrete level. Many books go straight to pictorial representations but students need plenty of opportunities to manipulate the models. They should use commercial ones, but they should also make their own individual sets of fraction squares, strips and circles. For the circles, it is best to cut out the paper copies so they make sure there are equal parts. Next, students should work on drawing their representations. This takes it to the next level of ownership of the internal knowledge of fractions. Finally, they should be doing abstract work with the symbols. Do not rush to the symbols. Teach fractions all year long through routines and energizers. In the beginning of the year be sure to do energizers and routines with the concepts they learned in first and second grade which is usually about halves, thirds and fourths.

Reflection Questions

1. How are you currently teaching fraction lessons?
2. Are you making sure that you do concrete, pictorial and abstract activities?
3. What do your students struggle with the most, and what ideas are you taking away from this chapter that might inform your work around those struggles?

References

Empson, S. B. (1999). Equal sharing and shared meaning: The development of fraction concepts in a first-grade classroom. *Cognition and Instruction, 17,* 283–342.

Fazio, L., & Siegler, R. (n.d.). *Teaching fractions.* International Academy of Education & International Bureau of Education.

Kentucky Department of Education. (2007). *Support materials for core content for assessment version 4.1 mathematics.* Retrieved January 15, 2017.

National Council of Teachers of Mathematics. (2007). *The learning of mathematics: 69th NCTM yearbook.* Reston, VA: National Council of Teachers of Mathematics.

Small, M. (2017). *Good questions: Great ways to differentiate math in the standards based classroom.* New York: Teachers College Press.

Vamvakoussi, X., & Vosniadou, S. (2010). How many decimals are there between two fractions? Aspects of secondary school students' understanding of rational numbers and their notation. *Cognition and Instruction, 28*(2), 181–209.

Webb, N. (2002). *An analysis of the alignment between mathematics standards and assessments for three states.* Paper presented at the annual meeting of the American Educational Research Association, New Orleans, LA.

9

Action Planning and FAQs

Well, to get started, you must get started. So, pick where you want to start and just begin. Begin small. Here is an Action Checklist (see Figure 9.1):

Figure 9.1

Before the Lesson	
Decide on the topic that you want to do.	
Why are you doing this topic?	
Is this emerging, on grade level or advanced?	
Map out a 3-cycle connected lesson plan.	
What are you going to do concretely?	
What are you going to do pictorially?	
What are you going to do abstractly?	
What misconceptions and error patterns do you anticipate?	
During the Lessons	
What are your questions?	
How are the students doing?	
What do you notice?	
What do you hear?	
What do you see?	
After the Lessons	
What went well?	
What will you tweak?	
What will you do the same?	
What will you do differently?	

DOI: 10.4324/9781003169543-9

What made you say "Wow!"	
What made you think "Uh-oh. . . ."	
What did you notice?	
What did you wonder?	
Other Comments	

Frequently Asked Questions

1. What Is a Guided Math Group?

Guided math is when you pull a temporary small group of students for instruction around a specific topic. Sometimes the groups are heterogeneous, and sometimes they are homogeneous. It depends on what you are teaching. If you are teaching a specific skill, like a strategy for adding multi-digit numbers and you have some students who know it and others who are struggling, then you would pull the students who need to learn it into a small group. However, sometimes you are working on general concepts, like modeling solving word problem with models. You can pull a heterogeneous group to teach this.

2. Why Do Guided Math?

You do guided math for a variety of reasons. Lillian Katz said it best:

> When a teacher tries to teach something to the entire class at the same time, chances are, one-third of the kids already know it; one-third will get it; and the remaining third won't. So two-thirds of the children are wasting their time.

You do guided math so that everyone gets to learn. You can pull students for remedial work, on grade level work and enrichment. You do guided math so that students understand the math they are doing. You work with students in small groups so that they can talk, understand, reason and do math!

3. What Are the Types of Lessons?

There are five types of guided math lessons: conceptual, procedural, reasoning, strategy and disposition. Mostly disposition lessons are integrated throughout the other lessons, but sometimes you just pull students and talk about their journey. That could look like, *what is tricky about what we are learning?* And, *what is easy?*

4. Do You Always Use Manipulatives in a Guided Math Group?

No. It depends where you are in the cycle of developing the concepts and student understanding. You certainly should use manipulatives in the beginning when you are developing concepts, but eventually when students are practicing at the abstract level, they probably won't be working directly with manipulatives, although, sometimes they still use them to check their answers or even solve problems if they need to.

5. What About Doing Worksheets in Guided Math Groups?

Never. It's simple. Guided math is students doing math, not doing a worksheet. Sometimes, you do pull students to work on some specific problems on a journal page but that is not the norm or the regular structure of a guided math group. Oftentimes when you are working through some problems in a journal which is mandated by some districts, you should scaffold the problems with manipulatives and templates so the students work on conceptual understanding.

Reference

Katz, L. Retrieved April 15, 2019 from www.azquotes.com/author/39264-Lilian_Katz